ALL ABOUT
THEM

ALL ABOUT
THEM

Grow Your Business by Focusing on Others

BRUCE TURKEL

Da Capo
LIFE
LONG

DA CAPO LIFELONG BOOKS

Copyright © 2016 by Bruce Turkel

All rights reserved. No part of this publication may be reproduced, stored in a retrieval system, or transmitted, in any form or by any means, electronic, mechanical, photocopying, recording, or otherwise, without the prior written permission of the publisher. Printed in the United States of America. For information, address Da Capo Press, 44 Farnsworth Street, 3rd Floor, Boston, MA 02210.

Designed by Linda Mark
Set in 12 point Bembo Std by Perseus Books

Cataloging-in-Publication data for this book is available from the Library of Congress.

First Da Capo Press edition 2016
ISBN: 978-0-7382-1920-2 (hardcover)
ISBN: 978-0-7382-1921-9 (e-book)

Published by Da Capo Press, an imprint of Perseus Books, a division of PBG Publishing, LLC, a subsidiary of Hachette Book Group, Inc.

Da Capo Press books are available at special discounts for bulk purchases in the U.S. by corporations, institutions, and other organizations. For more information, please contact the Special Markets Department at the Perseus Books Group, 2300 Chestnut Street, Suite 200, Philadelphia, PA 19103, or call (800) 810-4145, ext. 5000, or e-mail special.markets@perseusbooks.com.

10 9 8 7 6 5 4 3 2 1

To my mother, who inspired my love of writing and books.
With love and thanks.

CONTENTS

FOREWORD

GREAT SALESMANSHIP IS ABOUT THOSE YOU WISH TO lead, influence, and sell.

So it stands to reason that great product branding and marketing should be about them too.

What is branding about? The correct question is actually, *Who* is branding about? The answer: it's about those people whose lives you want to touch, whose lives you want to add exceptional value to, whose lives you want to help make better . . . *by way of* your products.

In other words, it's all about *them*!

That's the basic premise of this magnificent book by a true master of the game of branding and marketing. And you're about to learn that there is a proven, predictable, and duplicable way to win that game.

Bruce Turkel is a branding genius. He's worked with numerous major brands, ranging from 154-year-old Bacardi to the city of Miami, helping them to attract legions of new fans, reach their goals, and dramatically increase their profits.

Bruce has appeared on numerous network talk shows to explain how major companies, from Amazon to Zynga, can come back and repair their brands after making mistakes that did not honor their consumers. Bruce calls it "brand-aid."

Perhaps Bruce is best known to American viewers as the branding expert on Fox Business—and one of Melissa Francis and David Asman's favorite guests—having appeared well over three hundred times! Bruce accomplished this not just through being excellent at what he does but by knowing how to successfully position himself as the sought-after expert. And true to his creed, he doesn't make it about himself; he makes it about *them*—"them" in this case being his hosts *and* their viewers.

You see, we no longer control our brands. Perhaps we can manage them by what we do correctly. But it's not about us *or* our products. This can be very, very good. Or this can be very, very bad.

And that's why it's so important to approach branding as both an art and a science. Fortunately, our guide in this venture is both a branding artist and a branding scientist.

Some people are excellent practitioners. They can do something and do it phenomenally well. This does not mean that they can effectively teach it though, as is so often the case with the star athletes who make poor coaches and genius scholars who turn out to be ineffective professors. Sure, they deserve credit for their accomplishments, but they simply don't have the empathy or understanding to transmit their knowledge to those who do not possess their level of talent.

Others are excellent teachers. They manage to share information so as to instill it in others in both practical and inspirational ways. These teachers deserve much credit for the contributions they make to others' achievements, even though they themselves may not have attained similar success in their own endeavors.

And then there are the Bruce Turkels of the world. Few and far between, these people have taken their raw talent and then studied, learned, and practiced their craft until they've achieved excellence.

The difference with these performers, however, is that they are also able to teach their craft to others. And they do so in a way that others can achieve huge successes in their own right.

This is what Bruce offers us. Whether you are just beginning to make your way in the business world or are a highly experienced marketer of your products or services, whether you're about to launch a brand-new product or you've made some mistakes and need some serious brand-aid, you're now holding the roadmap to success beyond which you might have ever thought possible.

All About Them treats us to an understanding of human nature that will forever change the way you think about branding yourself and your business—almost as if David Ogilvy wrote *Freakonomics*.

The most emotionally fulfilling—and profitable—aspect of your business is when people think of you and your brand and feel that their lives are better as a result. The good news is that once you understand the concepts in *All About Them* and get your brand message successfully working for you, it will begin doing the heavy lifting, allowing you to focus on where you can add the most value to those you serve.

Read this book and apply the wisdom-filled teachings, and your chances of eliciting those kinds of feelings in others—and success in your business—are practically guaranteed.

I'm excited for you and for the journey you are about to take through the pages of this fantastic book.

Best regards,

BOB BURG

Coauthor of *The Go-Giver*
and *Adversaries into Allies*

PREFACE
THE BIRTH OF A BIG IDEA

IT WAS THE YEAR 2000, AND I FELT THAT EVERYTHING was going my way. My advertising and branding firm was doing well; we were picking up profitable business and doing great work. My family was healthy and happy, and my marriage was strong. Also my first book, *Brain Darts*, had just been published. And even before it came out, I had received an invitation to have a book signing at one of the most prestigious design conferences in the country. As I said, everything was going my way.

The day before the conference, my family and I checked into our Chicago hotel, and after getting the kids settled in our room, my wife and I went down to the opening dinner. When we got to the giant banquet hall, we were greeted like returning war heroes. The publisher of the design magazine sponsoring the event rushed over and escorted us to the VIP table all the way in the front of the hall, and I sat next to Steff Sagmeister. I don't know if you know Steff, but that year he was the "it boy" graphic designer. You know, just like Hollywood, the design industry has its "it" boys and girls. And that year, Steff, a tall, very handsome German guy dressed in all black, was "it." Because Steff was German, he spoke English better than I do, but he had managed to keep just enough of his accent to be charming.

It turned out Steff, like me, had just released a design book, and we were going to do our book signings together. But it gets better: seated on my other side, right next to my wife, was the chief marketing officer of one of the most design-forward corporations in the country—a major US company you'd instantly recognize if I told you the name—and a potential client I had lusted after for a long time. So, of course, I figured that after I finished my book signing and met all my new fans, I'd get the opportunity to pitch my firm to this guy and maybe get some work from his company.

Wow! Life was good.

The next morning I got up early and went downstairs to arrange everything just so. Estimating that I'd be signing a lot of books, I had bought a box of Sharpies, and I wanted all the books lined up neatly and within close reach to make it as easy as possible to satisfy the hordes of fans I knew would be rushing down to get their autographed copies.

After I'd arranged everything just the way I like it, I went for a run in the blustery Chicago morning. Even the cold wind blowing off the lake couldn't diminish my excitement, and I ran a bit faster and farther than usual.

Returning to the hotel with a tray of Starbucks coffee and scones for my family, I took a nice warm shower and got dressed. When it was time to head down to the book signing, my six-year-old daughter, Ali, asked if she could go with me.

My day was shaping up beautifully.

The elevator doors slid open, Ali took my hand, and we walked out to find a long line of people standing outside the expo hall, waiting for it to open and let them in for the book signing. Ali looked up at me and asked if all these people were waiting in line for my book. Sensing a teaching moment and not wanting to sound quite as full of myself as I felt, I told her that I was sure some of the people were in line for Steff's book too.

My daughter and I walked hand in hand past the line and into the expo center, where the line snaked around the trade show booths to the roped-off book signing tables all the way at the back of the room. We finally got to the end and turned the corner only to find that the entire line led to Steff's booth. There wasn't a single person waiting at mine.

Not one.

I walked behind my table and sat down, careful to not make eye contact with anyone standing in Steff's line. Ali busied herself drawing pictures with my exquisitely laid out Sharpies, while I tried in vain to use the Vulcan mind meld to will people to come up to my booth.

Every so often I would catch someone's eye, and that person would either look away quickly or give me what we in Miami call the *Pero que pobrecito* look, which for those of you who don't speak Spanish translates roughly to "You poor thing." It was a look of shame and pity mixed with a little embarrassment.

I didn't think I could feel any worse than I did at that moment. But I was wrong.

Because just then my six-year-old decided to take matters into her own hands. Ali jumped up from her folding chair, darted under the table, and popped out on the other side, running up to people in line, grabbing them by the hand, and saying, "Why don't you come look at my daddy's book? It's really good."

If I was getting *que pobrecito* looks before, hostile glares were now saying, "Get this little girl off me."

I didn't think I could feel any worse than I did at that moment. I was wrong again.

Because just then my beautiful wife came walking up, and she wasn't alone. You see, it turned out that she'd run into the great big, famous potential client at the breakfast buffet and convinced him to come with her to my triumphant book signing, promising him a free copy and the opportunity to talk to her brilliant designer superstar husband about his company's latest design project. She'd even told him they probably wouldn't have to wait in line.

Little did she know how very right she was about the waiting-in-line thing.

My wife and my potential dream client stood there dumbfounded, while I sat behind my piles of books and pens, watching my daughter trying to drag reluctant people over to my booth. By this time Steff had sold all of his books and was posing for photos with the hordes of grinning fans who had gotten one of his precious signed volumes.

At that moment I was too dejected and stunned to understand what had just happened. But I spent the next two years thinking about it and trying to figure out how to make sure that it never happened again. My experience that day and everything I've learned over subsequent days and years has helped me build a vibrant brand and a robust business. And that's what I want to share with you in this book. Because my road-to-Damascus moment, experienced in the back of an expo hall in some hotel in Chicago, taught me the most important thing I know about how to get ahead in business and life.

Let me share a few more details I didn't think were important at the time but became more and more vital the more I thought about the situation.

Remember how I told you that Steff and I were both invited to the conference before our books were released? This meant that the people waiting in line had never seen the contents of either my book or Steff's. Except for perhaps having glimpsed the odd article in some obscure design magazine, no one knew anything about either volume. They were queuing up to buy our products sight unseen.

To make matters worse, our big, beautiful coffee-table books were tightly bound in clear shrink-wrap plastic. The people waiting in line couldn't have looked inside if they wanted to. Even putting a few unwrapped books on the tables wouldn't have helped because Steff's line was too long to tolerate anyone standing there leisurely paging through his or my work. Talk about not judging a book by its cover: the covers really were the only input the people waiting in line had to guide their decision.

But the difference between our two books, besides the cover designs, was that Steff's was written by a known quantity, a celebrity even, and my book was written by a nobody. You see, I figured out years later that not one person at that design conference on that dreary day in Chicago was buying either one of our books because of their contents. They were buying a little piece of Steff. They most certainly were not buying a little bit of me. After all, I was a good designer, but Steff was a good designer with a strong brand and strong brand recognition. And that made all the difference in the world.

This simple little point, this seemingly obvious observation, was the bolt of lightning that changed how I looked at marketing and business and now informs how I market myself and run my own business. More, this little insight led to a comprehensive marketing strategy that ultimately led to my books and my blog, as well as my weekly appearances on national TV and the opportunities those activities have created for me.

The obvious takeaway would be that Steff sold more books simply because people knew who he was. In other words, the known quantity was a more compelling and comfortable purchase than the unknown one. But if that were all it took to succeed, then building a powerful brand and selling a greater number of products would be easy to accomplish through simple awareness. Study retail sales, however, and you'll see that this conclusion is incorrect. History is littered with the overabundant carcasses of well-known products that did not sell, effective politicians who didn't get elected, popular bands that fell out of favor, and once ubiquitous companies that no longer exist.

Sure, some products are relegated to the dust heap of irrelevance simply because they don't matter anymore. When was the last time you bought a buggy whip, an eight-track cassette player, a typewriter, or an 8-mm film projector? How about a calculator, a water bed, or an inkwell? Those products no longer exist (or exist only as oddities) because technology has given us better tools to accomplish their same tasks.

But plenty of brands that actually functioned as well as or better than the industry leader also wound up out of business. The VHS format outsold Betamax, even though experts all agree that the latter format was superior. Friendster gave way to MySpace, which in turn gave way to Facebook. And who's to say that by the time you are holding this volume, Facebook won't have been outpaced by its replacement too?

Does this suggest that my book was actually better than Steff's? Although I had no idea at the time (remember that Steff's book was wrapped in plastic, and I couldn't see inside), I do have to admit that once I got a chance to read his work, I saw that Steff had done a better job than I had. His book was spectacular. But at the time that was an irrelevant distinction and an unknowable difference. Neither volume was available for inspection by anyone waiting in line for a signature.

So if it was not simply a matter of awareness—that is, if it wasn't just that Steff was better known—and it wasn't only a matter of quality, what helped Steff's books fly off the shelves while mine lingered? What secret explains what happened? And more importantly, what discernable difference can you harness to build your business, improve your career, increase your sales, charge more for your products, and build your revenue?

For those looking to boost their personal brands and see their businesses flourish, *All About Them* answers those questions.

INTRODUCTION

FUNCTION HAS BECOME COST-OF-ENTRY— AND THAT SUCKS FOR YOU

The simple, universal truth is that in today's world of computerized production and globalized distribution, most products work even better than we expect them to. And if you do a little digging, you'll discover that many of the components that make up the many different products we purchase all come from the same factories or are at least built based on the same technology and the same patents to begin with. From automobiles to laptops to microwave ovens, one product's functionality is similar or identical to its competition's because its origins and components are as well.

CDs moved music from the analog to the digital environment. With the introduction of this new technology, all the problems associated with old (analog) record players disappeared, and pops, scratches, and hiss were all things of the past. Why? Because unlike analog recording, which loses quality and resolution with each pass, digital recording (e.g., duplicating a CD) is a "lossless procedure." In other words, a digital reproduction is actually a clone and not a copy of the original because it includes every bit of its parent's data. And while there may be many different recording formats, including .wav, .aif, .mp3, and .mp4 files, the information recorded in all of them is always digital, so reproduction imposes no degradation or information penalty.

Thanks to digital technology, then, the high-quality reproduction of music has become both generic and ubiquitous.

While we're talking about home entertainment, think about televisions for a moment. If you are old enough to remember what televisions looked like before flat screens, you're probably thinking of a big box, angled in the back to fit the picture tube, and maybe even a set so old that it had dials on the front to change the channels and adjust the volume.

Remember those dials? At some point the little gears inside them would strip, and they wouldn't be able to grip the little peg in the middle that changed the channels. That happened often enough that it wasn't odd to visit a friend and see a small pair of pliers or a Vice-Grip locked onto the little post where the dial used to be.

How about remote controls? Remember those strange little boxes with the big buttons sticking out of them? Unlike today's remotes, which do virtually everything but toast your bread and make your coffee in the morning, the early ones were only good for changing the channel and raising and lowering the volume. But sooner or later they'd stop working too, and the only way to change the channel would be to get up off the couch and walk across the room to the actual TV set. Believe it or not, the three networks operating at the time would schedule new or less popular shows after blockbuster hits because they knew that lots of viewers were too lazy to get up and change the channel and would therefore watch a program they wouldn't ordinarily choose.

Antennas (remember them?) would also break, and then the TV would be incapable of picking up the broadcast at all. Stores like Radio Shack did a brisk business selling replacement antennas, known as "rabbit ears." Most of the time, though, people would just replace the snapped off antenna with a wire clothes hanger bent in the same *V* shape as the original. This work-around didn't usually work very well, but then the TV's resolution and picture quality weren't that good to begin with.

Of course, the biggest problem with the old TVs was that eventually the picture tube would blow, and then the set would be completely worthless. Regardless of whether your dial dialed, your remote control controlled remotely, or your antenna had been replaced by a clothes hanger, once the tube blew, the old TV was a worthless piece of junk taking up space in your living room, and it was time to go out and buy a new set.

But after many years of development, televisions finally evolved to a level where they didn't break anymore. And this caused a big problem for television manufacturers. Because the TV market was mature, and most everyone who wanted a television already had one, there was simply no reason for anyone to purchase a new set.

The television industry overcame customers' purchase reluctance with technological innovation. TVs got bigger and bigger, screens got brighter and clearer, and the sound got better and better, incentivizing consumers to go out and buy new sets. Cable-ready and web-enabled boxes, DVRs, HiDef, and smart TVs were just a few of the many leaps in the technological race that gave consumers and retailers an entirely new way of looking at, thinking about, and purchasing televisions. Thanks to flat-screen technology, consumers were able to buy larger and larger sets and mount them on their walls, finally making high-quality home theaters possible even for budget-conscious buyers.

A few years after flat screens became ubiquitous, my wife and I redid our house. While we were replacing the drywall in our family room and bedrooms, we decided to run the wires so that we too could install flat-screen sets. And that meant that our old TVs, a big Sony Trinitron and an even larger JVC, had to go.

I got up on a chair and pulled the TVs' cartons out of our storage space and repackaged the sets in their original boxes, complete with the Styrofoam packing material and their original manuals in the little bags they came in. Believe it or not, I still had the little batteries for the remote controls lying in their little plastic bags, secured with their own tiny little staples.

But what was I going to do with these two old but perfectly preserved televisions? I offered them to the guy who mows our lawn, but he didn't want them. I offered them to the mechanic who keeps my old car running. He didn't want them either. I addressed an e-mail to "everybody," the distribution list for all the people who work in my company, offering the two televisions on a first-come-first-served basis to whoever wanted them. No one even responded.

Because we were doing all this work around our house, we had collected bags of things we didn't want or need anymore:

clothes that had been out of style for years, equipment for sports our kids didn't play anymore, chipped pottery, broken records, and all the other things that had filled our drawers and closets for years and years.

I loaded them all into boxes and slid them into the back of my wife's SUV. Then I hitched on the bicycle rack and went looking for my kids' old bikes. I found them leaning against the chain link fence over by the garbage cans—rusty old bicycles that my kids had jumped off of one day and left outside to weather the elements. It was no surprise that they'd never been stolen. Who would have wanted them?

I hoisted the bikes up onto the rack and drove to the nearest Goodwill center to unload my stash.

The woman manning the Goodwill happily showed me where to park the rusty bikes and pointed to the dolly she wanted me to use to move the cartons to the corner of the backroom. It wasn't until I reached into the car to pull out the TV boxes that she protested.

"No sir, not those. We don't take old TVs."

I was surprised at her outburst but quickly assumed that it was because the woman didn't know my TVs were in perfect condition. After all, Goodwill probably didn't want to be the collection point for piles of broken televisions that they would just have to throw away after their donors had left.

"Oh, don't worry," I assured her. "These TVs work perfectly. Look, I even have the manuals and the remote controls. If you have an outlet somewhere, I'll plug them in and show you."

"Sir," she answered, clearly annoyed, "we don't want your old TVs."

"But these are perfect," I protested. "Someone will want them. They're great TVs."

"Sir," she repeated, more annoyed this time, "no one wants them. Even poor people have flat screens!"

How I finally got rid of those old TVs doesn't really matter, but what I learned matters a lot. My experience with those perfectly good televisions opened my eyes to a new idea: in a society and time where most everything works, function has become cost-of-entry. Consumers, even those with limited means who shopped at Goodwill to save money, weren't just choosing products for what they could accomplish; they were choosing them for what they said about the purchaser. Perfectly good televisions weren't good enough. People needed something more.

If all products and services work equally well, or at least appear to, then that very functionality becomes an expected commodity. What used to be the paramount feature of a product—how well it worked—is no longer an important part of a consumer's consideration set because they can find the same quality anywhere. Instead, a new mantra has arisen that explains how and why consumers buy in today's hyper-efficient, hyperconnected society: people don't choose what you do; they choose who you are.

In other words, when all products are similarly functional and acceptable, it's the way a product makes you feel, not the way it works, that matters.

This means that whether or not Steff's book was better than mine was ultimately irrelevant. For whatever reason—his celebrity (remember, he was the design industry's "it boy" that year), his good looks, his charm, his history of groundbreaking work, his reputation, his list of industry awards—the attendees at the design conference felt better about themselves because they had a little piece of Steff. Carrying his signed book under their arms made them feel good and made them feel good about themselves. They had touched the celebrity fire and lived to tell about it.

Because the attendees at the design conference had never heard of me or my company, my book was just a book, another functional device for them to read and store on their bookshelves. But Steff's book was so much more than a book because of all of the good feelings that came along with it. Like hanging a new flat-screen television on the wall, displaying Steff's book on their coffee tables showed they had a keepsake, a souvenir of their experience, to savor later.

ECO-FRIENDLY AND PROUD OF IT

In 2003 Toyota released its second-generation hybrid, the Prius, in the United States. According to Wikipedia,

> Global cumulative (Toyota) Prius sales reached the milestone one million vehicle mark in May 2008, two million in September 2010, and passed the three million mark in June 2013. Cumulative sales of one million were achieved in the U.S. by early April 2011, and Japan reached the one million mark in August 2011.

But back when the second-generation Prii were released, none of this success was assured or even expected. The first-generation Prius was released in the US in 1997 and marketed as the world's first mass-produced gasoline-electric hybrid car. With a new nameplate attached to an unremarkable design, Toyota's first-generation Prius was not only a lackluster performer on the road but also at the dealerships, where only 123,000 units sold worldwide between 1997 and 2001.

But that was before the completely redesigned second-generation Prius.

You might remember that when first released, Toyota's hybrid wedge became the instant darling of the Hollywood elite: Gwyneth Paltrow, Kate Hudson, Orlando Bloom, Natalie Portman, Cameron Diaz, and even Harrison Ford were all seen driving theirs around Los Angeles. All of a sudden, a Prius was more than a car. It was a bold statement that told the world its driver was a sensitive world citizen who cared deeply about the environment. The statement was so bold, in fact, that between the second-generation model's introduction in 2003 and its redesign in 2009, Toyota sold about 1.192 million second-generation Prii around the world, almost five times as many as it had of the first-generation car. And through September 2014, Toyota sold over 3.250 million of its second- and third-generation Prius Hybrids.

Interestingly, around the same time that Toyota found such great success with the Prius, Honda introduced its Civic Hybrid. While the specs of the two cars may have been similar, Honda did not design an entirely new automobile; instead it created a hybrid version of its very popular Civic. In fact, except for a few detail changes and the addition of six letters to the model name, the standard edition Civic and the Civic Hybrid were virtually and visually indistinguishable.

Unfortunately for Honda, Hollywood's superstars did not instantly adopt the Civic Hybrid as their auto du jour as they had with Toyota's little Prius, and neither did the general public. The proof is in the sales numbers: by 2009 Honda had sold only 255,249 Civic Hybrids and moved less than 30,000 units in the United States in 2012 and 2013, whereas the Prius is now in its third iteration, and since 2011 the latest model alone has sold 853,834 units.

But if hybrids in general were so popular because of their increased fuel mileage and decreased emissions, why weren't Honda's sales nearly as robust as Toyota's?

Unlike the equally efficient but unremarkable-looking Honda Civic Hybrid, the uniquely shaped Prius announced to the world that it was a special car for special people. The prosaic Honda merely said, "I'm driving a cheap car." Honda had created a functionally equivalent car but dropped the ball when it came to designing the look of the vehicle. The car's style did nothing to make its drivers feel good about themselves.

In July 2007 the *New York Times* quoted a CNW Marketing Research finding that 57 percent of Prius buyers said their main reason for their purchase was that "it makes a statement about me," while only 37 percent cited fuel economy as their prime motivator. Shortly afterward, *Washington Post* columnist Robert Samuelson coined the term "Prius politics" to describe a situation where the driver's desire to "show off" is a stronger motivator than the desire to curb greenhouse gas emissions. Former Central Intelligence Agency (CIA) chief R. James Woolsey Jr. even went so far as to say that because oil profits find their way to terrorist groups like al-Qaeda,

Americans who bought inefficient vehicles would, in effect, be indirectly funding terrorism. "We're paying for both sides in this war, and that's not a good long-term strategy," said Woolsey. "I have a bumper sticker on the back of my Prius that reads, 'Bin Laden hates this car.'"

Imagine! Not only does driving a Toyota Prius tell the world that the person behind the wheel is socially and environmentally conscious, but according to CIA chief Woolsey, not doing so suggests that the driver supports terrorism. Quite a big responsibility for such a little car. Clearly the *Washington Post* was right when it dubbed hybrids "Hollywood's latest politically correct status symbol."

THE SECRET TO WRITING YOUR RÉSUMÉ AND GETTING A JOB

Do you remember your first résumé, the one you typed up when you went out to get your first real job? If you went job searching before the computer revolution, you probably had it printed up at a type shop or copy center. If you looked for your first job after personal computers showed up on everyone's desk, you most likely created it on-screen and printed it out on your laser printer. Regardless of how you created it, your first paragraph probably read something like this:

> I am endeavoring to find a uniquely creative opportunity with a successful and forward-thinking company where I can utilize my skills to their fullest potential and find significant opportunities for both professional advancement and personal fulfillment.

Okay, I'm sure your statement of objective differed slightly from my re-creation, but not by much. And my point still stands: most first-time résumés are written for the job seeker, not for the person who really matters: the person making the hiring decision.

Regardless of how many times your grandmother told you that you're the most important human being on the entire planet, the person reading the résumé couldn't care less about who you are or what you want. He is only interested in how well you will fill the open position and meet his needs.

If you're looking for a job at a large company, then a division head or a worker in the human resources department will probably read your résumé. And do you think those people care how much you want to become a copywriter, copy machine salesman, or accounting clerk? Of course not. They just want to find someone with all the qualifications the company is looking for who can start work immediately. Most importantly, the people reading your résumé are looking for someone who can make them look good. They want their supervisors to compliment them for the good hire so that they can enjoy their own opportunities for advancement. Your career path is the last thing on their minds except in terms of how it will affect and enhance their own goals.

That's important enough to repeat: your career is unimportant to them except as it affects theirs.

If you're applying to a smaller or more entrepreneurial company, the owner, a partner, or the chief financial officer will most likely review your résumé. These individuals care most about whether you can start making money for them right away. Small business owners and entrepreneurs are much more interested in your attitude and ability than in your interests, desires, hopes, or dreams. Once again, the message that matters most is what you are going to do for them, not what they're going to do for you.

So what will make a difference? How can you break the seemingly endless chain of ineffective résumés and cut through the clutter to increase the chance that your job application won't end up in the "Don't call us—we'll call you" file alongside so many others?

To find out, I spoke to University of Miami professor Mark Levit. Mark was a successful advertising agency owner in New York until he traded the subway for the sunshine and moved to South Florida. Today Mark teaches advertising and marketing and works with hundreds of students. Although his job description says that he teaches them about his former industry, he spends a lot more of his time trying to prepare his students for their first all-important job search.

Mark believes that the only statements worth making in a résumé's first paragraph promise readers that you will save them time, effort, or money or that you will make them money. Everything else, he says, is superfluous. "The person reading the résumé doesn't look at a student's job search the way the student does. They're scanning the document for key words signaling the applicant understands why they're being hired and what's expected of them. If they find that, then they'll go on to look at the applicant's specific qualifications. If they don't find it in the application, then the résumé goes directly to the circular file."

To misquote the late president John F. Kennedy, "State not what your company can do for you, state what you can do for your company."

Mark points out that because of the vast volume of résumés most employers receive, the task isn't always to find the best applicant in the bunch but instead to winnow the pile of applications to a moderately manageable stack. Anything that gives the screener an excuse to cull an applicant's letter or résumé will be used to eliminate it. "Of course typos are the kiss of death," Mark says. "But so are misaligned objectives, poorly communicated experiences, and nonspecific statements. The folks reading these documents are ruthlessly efficient. Remember that their job is to find the best applicant, not to give everyone a fair hearing. And it's most certainly not to hire you."

Thanks to helping his students write thousands of résumés and then tracking their successes and failures, Mark believes the ultimate résumé objective statement reads something like this:

> Being a successful [specific position title here] is the most important thing in the world to me. I will work 24/7 and do everything in my power to save you time, money, and effort and prove worthy of the confidence you have shown in me. I guarantee that you will not be disappointed.

"Students almost never put themselves in the shoes of their potential employers," Mark laments:

> If they did, I'm sure they would approach the whole job search activity with a very different attitude.
> What I mostly see, even from bright, concerned students is that they try to truly express themselves in their résumés. What they don't realize is that a résumé is the wrong place

to be yourself. Instead, it's the opportunity to be what the employer wants you to be. I'm not suggesting that my students should lie or even exaggerate—remember that in today's world, confirmation of a job prospect's former employment and education is only a mouse click away. What students need to do is look at their job search materials less as an opportunity to tell the world who they are and more as the chance to tell a potential employer what they can do for them.

That's what gets kids hired.

THE MOST IMPORTANT JOB IN THE WORLD

It's not just recent college graduates who need to create résumés (or brands) that talk specifically to their potential employers. Mark's suggestions don't work only for students looking for their first job; they are just as critical as one climbs the ladder. In fact, Mark's admonitions get more and more important the higher you climb, all the way up to the most important job in the world.

In 2008, when Americans went to the polls to pick the next president of the United States, their choices were pretty clear-cut. On the one side was Republican John McCain, a former war hero and a career politician. On the other side was the Democratic Party candidate, a virtually unknown community activist and short-time senator with the unlikely name of Barack Hussein Obama. Never before had there been such a clear choice for voters.

For the uninitiated, the race started out clearly in McCain's favor: he was already famous and met most of the criteria for previous American presidents. On paper, John McCain looked like he would be the next president of the United States. And based on the oft-repeated five *P*s of marketing—product, price, positioning, packaging, and promotion—it shouldn't have even been a contest.

The five *P*s of marketing provide a way to create a mix of disciplines and decisions that help marketers best reach their audiences. Research on the subject will reveal a number of different combinations in the mix itself. Some professionals talk about the four *P*s: price, product, promotion, and place. Others list as many as seven *P*s. But regardless of which theory you prefer, you'll find the classifications help determine how a product should be marketed and what makes purchasers respond most favorably.

Let's break down the five *P*s and see how the candidates faired:

1. PRODUCT

If we're completely honest, McCain was the product that most matched what we were used to seeing in the oval office. Even his name sounded like those of earlier presidents. John McCain's name sounds like George Bush's, whose name sounds like Bill Clinton's, whose name sounds like John Kennedy's, whose name sounds like Thomas Jefferson's, whose name sounds like George Washington's.

Barack Hussein Obama, on the other hand? Not exactly the kind of name we're used to, is it? Barack does mean "blessing" in Hebrew, but that's not something most Americans would know.

Let's do a little experiment: If I asked you to list the top one hundred names for an American president, would Hussein make the list? How about if I let you list two hundred names? How about five hundred? Chances are that people would never have listed the name Hussein if they were trying to name an American president, no matter how many options they were given.

And his last name: Obama? As his opponents continually told us, Obama rhymed with Osama, the first name of Osama bin Laden, America's public enemy number one. Even theoretically unbiased newscasters would often slip up and call the Democratic nominee for president "Osama."

Point one goes to McCain.

2. PRICE

In the marketing world, price stands for the price of a product. Once the brand is established and the customer is interested, then price has much to do with the ultimate purchase decision. The intuitive logic is that customers will always buy at a lower price, but this isn't true. The value of many products actually increases with increasing price. Consultants, perfume, and engagement rings are all examples of this seemingly backward pricing phenomenon.

But in the political arena, all products (or candidates) cost the same at the place of purchase (the polling place). Each shopper (voter) has a limited resource (one vote) to spend (cast) on his or her choice for president. And so instead of price standing for the cost of purchase, I've used it here to stand for budget: the amount of money that each candidate had available to advertise and promote his brand. At the time, by the way, the McCain/Obama fight for the 2008 presidential election was the most expensive in American history.

With all of that being said, this should have been an easy win for McCain. He had the history, the connections, the fund-raising experience, and the potential to raise considerably more money than Obama. But Obama's team exploited its understanding of nascent Internet technology, while the Republican candidate stuck to the old tried-and-true (and now irrelevant) fund-raising practices of most every election that had come before. In the end, Obama raised $760,370,195, more than twice as much as McCain's $358,008,447, or $10.94 per vote to McCain's $5.97.

But the story doesn't stop there because the candidates are not the only ones who spend on their campaigns. When you factor in the parties' contributions, you find that the Democratic National Committee took in over $206 million, while the Republican National Committee took in $337 million.

Based on spending, point two goes to Obama, whose total campaign resources were nearly $250 million more than McCain's.

3. POSITIONING

Here the advantage would have to go to McCain. He began his political career as a congressman in the US House in 1982, serving in that position until he was elected to the Senate in 1986. Because of all his political service, McCain had been in the public eye for more than a quarter century. The senator was well known and easily recognizable to politically savvy American voters.

And, of course, before entering politics, McCain had been a patriotic Vietnam War veteran who spent five years as a prisoner of war. The story of his capture and captivity in Vietnam was well known and well respected.

Obama, on the other hand, had been a senator for only a short period when he resigned his office to run for president. Before his time in the US Senate, he was described as a "community activist." You can choose whether that title is complimentary or not, but the simple truth is that the word "community" suggests that he worked in a small fishbowl and wasn't well known.

Point three, then, goes to McCain.

4. PACKAGING

If we can avoid the limited view that political correctness imposes, it's pretty easy to admit that Obama did not look like any president we'd seen before. And while his skin color was certainly an advantage in the eyes of some percentage of the electorate, honesty forces us to admit that it was probably not an asset in the overall.

Spend time at the Hall of Presidents at Disney World in Orlando, and you'll pretty quickly see that all of the animatic figures of former US presidents have a few things in common. Browse the portraits of the presidents hanging in the National Gallery in Washington, DC, and you'll find the same commonalities. Most notably, the presidents depicted are all male, they're all middle-aged or older, and they're all white. Obama fits the first two criteria but certainly not the third. As you walk out, you might be whistling the *Sesame Street* jingle "One of these things is not like the others. One of these things does not belong." The bottom line is that Obama simply did not look the way we expected an American president to look. And even though many of us grew up being told, "In America, anyone can grow up to be president," experience said otherwise, as all forty-three of the previous presidents of the United States shared common demographic traits.

Like it or not, point four goes to McCain, who is now winning three to one.

5. PROMOTION

Ah, here's where the rubber meets the road, because here is where Barack Hussein Obama overcame his losses in the other areas and definitively pulled away from John McCain and won the presidency. Quite simply, McCain clumsily built a campaign that was all about himself, while Obama's marketing team crafted one that resonated with voters.

McCain's campaign tagline, a succinct description of what a candidate stands for, was "I am a Maverick." Unfortunately for the McCain campaign, this fell short on a couple of levels. First, for a slightly older than middle-aged white man—and a former military officer at that—the term "maverick" was incongruous at best. McCain was anything but a maverick: he was a solid, middle-of-the-road to right-wing Republican. Yes, he'd been obstreperous in the Senate and had taken some less than popular positions from time to time, including partnering with Senator Russ Feingold, a liberal Democrat from Wisconsin, to author the campaign finance reform bill that shares their names. But to suggest that those stands qualified

McCain as a maverick pushed the bounds of credulity and contrasted unrealistically with his actual persona.

Second, "I am a Maverick" talked about who McCain was but said nothing about what that meant for the voting public. Sure, one could extrapolate that a maverick would do new and interesting things, but again, voters' experiences with McCain did not jibe with that definition.

Obama, on the other hand, presented his candidacy to the public with a motto that I believe will be recognized as one of the best advertising lines of all time, a simple three-word phrase that defined his presidency: "Yes we can."

"Yes" is positive.
"We" is inclusive.
"Can" is aspirational.

"Yes we can" told potential voters that together we could accomplish great things. It didn't specifically say what any of those things would be, but it included us in the good works that were going to occur with Obama's presidency. "Yes we can" promised us that we Americans would make great things happen.

Did it work? Well the proof is in the results. Not only did a majority of American voters pick Obama to be their next president, but 68 percent—two-thirds—of first-time voters chose him as well. It's particularly interesting that the line had its greatest influence on first-time voters because you can argue that they were least aware of the issues. Instead, they responded to a brand message that not only included them but also made them feel good about the things that were about to happen. As we will discuss in detail later, *good brands make you feel good, but great brands make you feel good about yourself.* The line "Yes we can" did exactly that for young voters.

Now, before you think I'm taking sides here, let's see what happened after the election was over and Obama the visionary became Obama the functionary. Almost immediately after his inauguration, President Obama stopped communicating as effectively as candidate Obama had. In fact, on his signature issue—health care—the new president completely failed to frame the argument in a compelling manner, instead allowing Congress, the pundits, and even his adversaries to define his health-care initiative.

One of the truest axioms of politics is that it's crucial to define yourself and your programs before your opponent does. And nowhere is the law of physics that nature abhors a vacuum truer than in the world of politics. Because the president himself did not craft the defining tagline for his signature health-care plan, he unwittingly allowed a Republican senator from Iowa to shape the message for him. Chuck Grassley's five-word phrase "pulling the plug on grandma" was so effective and convincing that it nearly scuttled the health-care bill altogether.

What's more, former Alaska governor and vice presidential candidate Sarah Palin took to Facebook to demonize one component of the Affordable Care Act as "death panels." Ironically, Grassley's and Palin's statements both referred to end-of-life discussions that had actually been among former president George W. Bush's health-care suggestions. Regardless, due to Grassley's and Palin's reframing of Obama's program, the new president's signature bill almost went down in flames. And even though his plan was eventually voted into law, the Affordable Care Act (or ObamaCare) was presented to the American people as an eviscerated program with much of its substance left on the cutting room floor during the ensuing debate.

Grassley and Palin understood very well that while most voters and constituents would never read or comprehend the thousands of pages of health-care policy under debate, a simple, emotional message expressing exactly how the plan would affect people's lives could swing public sentiment against the legislation. "Pulling the plug on grandma" made a very clear statement about what would happen if the bill were voted into law. The image of death panels quickly put a macabre face on an otherwise bureaucratic and uninteresting governmental organization.

Grassley and Palin had figured out how to communicate what they wanted their constituencies to believe—and, more importantly, to feel—about President Obama's proposed health-care bill, and their interpretations, wrapped in powerfully emotional messages, hit home.

TYING IT ALL TOGETHER

So far we've looked at an interesting but seemingly disjointed list of experiences. What do used televisions, Toyota's Prius Hybrid, professor Mark Levit's course on successful résumé writing, Palin and Grassley's anti-ObamaCare messages, and the 2008 presidential election all have in common? And remember my first book signing, discussed in the preface? What did I learn from that disastrous experience that changed my business, my way of dealing with people, and my life?

More importantly, what can you learn from all this?

Simply put, the most successful brand messages are All About Them.

As you'll see, the most powerful, compelling marketing messages and brand identities are not about the companies or individuals they are promoting but about the people they are trying to reach. More to the point, they're about making the target consumers feel good about themselves because of their interaction with the brand.

Owning a signed copy of Steff's book let designers and design fans feel good about themselves and their experience at the creativity conference. President Obama was elected because his message, "Yes we can," was affirmative, inclusive, and positive and honored the people he was trying to persuade to vote for him. Senator Grassley's and former governor Palin's messages nearly derailed the Affordable Care Act because they offered voters what Obama never did: a direct emotional appeal that explained their view of what ObamaCare would mean for them. Mark Levit's best students' résumés go against the grain because they don't concentrate on the qualifications of the job applicant but instead inform and reassure potential bosses that their companies and lives will be better if they hire the résumé writer.

Although you could argue that Toyota's Prius Hybrid didn't offer drivers any discernably different functional benefits from its most direct competition, the unique design of the car broadcast its driver's concern for the environment. While the Honda Civic Hybrid said, "I'm cheap," the Toyota Prius Hybrid said, "I care." And while a state-of-the-art flat-screen TV might have more bells and whistles than the older and larger technology, the viewing experience is arguably similar. But the newer flat screens also provide an image of status and affluence that lower-income consumers appreciate.

That's the pure power of All About Them. It cuts through the clutter and immediately informs your listeners that what you have to say is important to them. It often obviates facts and figures because it gets right to the heart of what matters to consumers: their own self-interest.

Here's the ugly little secret about human behavior and the best marketing that takes advantage of it: people are most concerned with themselves. And while this seems obvious, I never cease to wonder at how people forget this simple tenet and instead fill their marketing with superfluous facts and figures that only obscure the true message the advertiser is trying to communicate in the first place.

I'm sorry to say that you've done it too.

And that's what this book is all about: showing you exactly how to harness the sheer power of All About Them to get your point across and convince your customers to see things from your point of view.

1

NOBODY'S HAPPY

THE GRANDMOTHER AND THE LIFEGUARD

The old woman was running along the shoreline.

"My grandson, my grandson, he's drowning! Help!" she shrieked.

The lifeguard heard the old woman's pleas and jumped off his stand. He plunged into the water and searched around desperately until he found the small body thrashing under the surf. Ignoring the dangerous undertow, the lifeguard dove down and grabbed the little boy. When he had a good grip around the boy's chest, he changed direction and kicked up to the surface fighting the surf the whole way.

Exhausted and out of breath, the lifeguard pulled the boy through the crashing waves and onto the beach. He dropped to his knees and performed mouth-to-mouth resuscitation, alternately breathing into the little boy's mouth and pressing on his chest. Five excruciating minutes passed before the boy suddenly convulsed, coughed up a lungful of water, and started breathing on his own.

The exhausted lifeguard caught his own breath and looked up at the old woman.

"Your grandson is alive," he gasped. "Everything will be fine."

The old woman looked at the lifeguard, then at the little boy, and then at the lifeguard again before speaking.

"He had a hat."

HOW WE WERE, HOW WE HAVE CHANGED

Like every other baby boomer growing up in the 1960s and 1970s, I was a kid back in the dark ages of transistor radios. If a friend told me about a cool new song that I had to hear, I'd tune in to WQAM and wait for it to come on. If the song was hot, I'd have to wait about an hour or so, but if it wasn't, I could still be waiting well past my bedtime. While I waited I'd get my cassette recorder plugged in and loaded so I could tape the song to listen to it again and again and share with my friends. But invariably I'd miss the beginning and inadvertently record my mom calling me to dinner in the middle of one of the verses. It was almost impossible to get a usable recording of a favorite song unless I went to the record store and bought the album. But even if I had the money and a ride to the store, I still couldn't just buy the song I liked; I had to buy the whole record or at least the 45 RPM single, which still came with a B-side track.

Sometimes I had a little allowance money burning a hole in my pocket and wanted to order something from the ads on the back of my comic books: sea monkeys, say, or X-ray specs. But purchasing something from a mail-order company was even harder than getting over to the record store to buy a new song. First I'd have to convince my mom that I really should buy the item. Then I'd have to get her to write a check, put it in an envelope, and root around for a stamp. Then I'd bicycle down the street to the mailbox to send off my order. But even after all that, I'd still have to wait the dreaded four to six weeks that the small print in the comic book ad had warned me about.

Of course four to six weeks is an eternity to a twelve-year-old, and a day or two after I mailed my order, I'd start religiously checking the mailbox every day after school. As with the proverbial watched pot that doesn't boil, my excited attention didn't make the package arrive any sooner either.

Wow, have things changed. Today when my daughter gets a text message from her BFF about a great new band she has to hear, an MP4 file of the actual song usually accompanies the SMS. If not, she can go to YouTube or the iTunes Store, download the song to her phone, and listen to it right away.

If my son wants to buy something, he can simply order it online and have it FedEx'd to him in a day or two. And while he waits he can track his package as it wings its way across the country. No one over forty-five years old actually cares where the package is until it arrives in his or her hot little hands, but younger consumers need to follow it every step of the journey. They want to know when it's in Tulsa, when it's in Memphis, and when it's on the delivery truck (just as I paced around the mailbox waiting for my sea monkeys—some things never change regardless of the technology.)

Of course, if it's a book he wants, he can just one-click-order it on Amazon and have it transmitted to his Kindle, iPad, smartphone, or laptop in less than sixty seconds. And if he's stuck somewhere without one of his gizmos, he can just dial the book up in the Kindle app on whatever digital device he has with him, and the system will not only locate the book but set the digital bookmark at wherever he last stopped reading.

"I want it now" buyers like my children are labeled by a lot of names these days: Generation X, Generation Y, Echo Boomers, Millennials—demographic labels based on when they were born. But it would be more accurate to title them by their psychographic attributes, based on the one trait they all share: their addiction to instant gratification. These consumers are the Instant-On generation: young buyers who have grown up with the "What have you done for me next" demands of digital technology and have never had to function in an analog environment that does not immediately respond to their every want and whim.

Instant-Ons are the people you see at every red light reaching for their smartphones to check for e-mails or texts even though they just checked at the stoplight two blocks back. They're the impatient travelers rolling their eyes at the person in the airport security line who takes an extra minute to greet the TSA inspector. They're the ones tapping their phones for faster connections and cursing the slow Wi-Fi connections in hotel lobbies.

In short, Instant-Ons have never had to wait for anything and consequently suffer from severely atrophied attention spans.

Unfortunately for Instant-Ons, world events are conspiring to make things very difficult for them. Thanks to the combined effects of a burgeoning world population, expanded financial opportunity in the underdeveloped world, and the democratization of technology, there are more people on airplanes, more people in restaurants, more people consuming natural and man-made resources, and more people using technology to service far-off clients than ever before. And while Instant-Ons are perfectly happy to zoom along in their digital environments, finding their friends on Foursquare, making reservations via OpenTable, and communicating with each other 24/7/365 across Facebook, Twitter, and WhatsApp, the sheer number of people expecting immediate service in the carbon universe amounts to an unscalable goat rodeo that slows everything down.

Before you start pining for the good old days, remember that things weren't that slow before. It's just that there were far fewer people clamoring for service, and those people were way more willing to wait their turn. But older consumers didn't grow up with the instant reward and response of video games. They didn't grow up with the instant gratification of flash-frozen prepared foods heated in a microwave. And they didn't grow up with 24/7/365 communication devices glowing greedily in their pockets and demanding constant attention.

Today's Instant-On consumer did, however, and today's marketer is going to have to figure out how to successfully serve people who live the lyrics to the Queen song—"I want it all and I want it now"—as if the rock opera were a real-life scenario.

Talking about today's sped-up world, taciturn comedian Steven Wright quipped, "If you put instant coffee in a microwave you almost go back in time." But the funny thing here is, I don't smell coffee—I smell opportunity. Specifically, I smell opportunities for companies and entrepreneurs to figure out how to satisfy Instant-Ons, the consumers who don't have the time or focus to be satisfied with anything.

Improved customer experience is one such opportunity: think of Disney World's line-management techniques or the TSA security experience at Las Vegas's McCarran Airport. In Miami, wealthy wannabe Latin American Instant-Ons can hire people to stand in line for them at immigration. And each time Apple releases a new version of the iPhone, people show up early to queue up, only to sell their spots to affluent Johnny-come-latelys who would rather pay than actually wait in line.

In fact, Bloomberg reported that more than two hundred people in New York and San Francisco got paid to stand in the queue for buyers of Apple's new iPhone 5—at the time the biggest consumer electronics debut in history. Furthermore, technology facilitated the transaction: "These arrangements were made on the website TaskRabbit, where a user can find someone to complete odd jobs such as assembling Ikea furniture or, in this case, waiting in long lines."

But all of these solutions are just Band-Aids—quick solutions to little problems. The true moneymakers will be those who figure out how to reconcile Instant-Ons' digital expectations with analog reality in every mundane part of their lives.

For example, Google, Tesla, BMW, Mercedes, Audi, and Apple are all confirmed or rumored to be working on self-driving cars. And the technology will supposedly be ready for consumers sometime in the early 2020s, although in December 2014 the website ExtremeTech reported, "Google has [already] unveiled the first fully working road-legal prototype of its self-driving car." What's more, the site states, "If all goes to plan, Google hopes to partner with a real car maker to bring a self-driving vehicle to market in the next five years."

Think about the opportunities that self-driving cars will create to market to Instant-Ons. Besides the regular time we spend in our cars, already estimated at over one hundred hours per year, the *Atlantic* reports that traffic jams add an additional thirty-eight hours per commuter per year, with as much as sixty-one extra hours per year in Los Angeles and sixty-seven extra hours per year for drivers in Washington, DC. Of course, once self-driving cars are introduced, all of that time will be available for consumers to focus on other activities, and consuming advertised media will be one of the biggest (hence Google's keen interest, by the way).

FIRST WORLD PROBLEMS

The term "First World problems" first appeared in a 1979 article by G. K. Payne in *Built Environment*, but it gained significant popularity in 2005 as a social media response to trivial problems expressed by Instant-Ons and other people spoiled by affluence and technology. The term made its way into the *Oxford English Dictionary Online* in November 2012.

First World problems, more seriously referred to as the fallacy of relative privation, are a real concern for businesses, because in a world where consumers are never happy, it becomes more and more difficult to satisfy them.

Think back twenty years, to before you had ever heard of First World problems.

You had just checked into your hotel. You went up to your room, dropped your bags on the bed, and opened the drapes to enjoy your view. Then you walked into the bathroom and found a disgustingly large cockroach scrabbling around in your bathtub.

After you screamed or screeched or hopped up on the toilet tank, what did you do? Chances are you called the front desk and had Reception send somebody up to get rid of the giant bug.

But when your trip was over and you got home, you were still annoyed, so you decided to write a note and complain to the hotel. You dragged out your stationery, found a pen, scribbled your complaint, stuck it in an envelope, licked the flap, and searched around for a stamp.

Three weeks later the letter was still sitting on your mantle until you finally remembered to take it with you and drop it in a mailbox.

Three weeks after that (almost two months after your trip) you received a letter on the hotel's engraved stationery that said something like this:

Dear Sir or Madam,

We are so sorry you were not entirely satisfied with your stay at the XYZ Hotel. Thank you so much for bringing this unfortunate happenstance to our attention. Let us assure you that we are doing everything in our power to rectify this situation and to make sure it doesn't happen again.

Sincerely,
The Management

And that was it. Sure, you could have complained to a friend or two, but what difference would it have made? The situation was over.

Ten years ago, if you happened on the same roach in your hotel tub, you would have waited until you got home, fired up the computer, and zipped off an e-mail explaining your disappointment. And within a few days you probably would have received an e-mail reply that said pretty much the same thing as the letter.

Five years ago you would have sent the e-mail from your laptop or tablet and received a response while you were still in the hotel. Maybe the manager would even have sent up a bottle of wine and a hand-written note with his or her apologies.

Now think about what would happen today.

You walk into the bathroom and find the same damn roach partying in your tub. What's the first thing you do? Scream? No, you take a picture of the bug with your smartphone. And let's face it, you don't even have to reach for your phone because it is already in your hand because you were either texting a buddy or playing Candy Crush or Words with Friends as you walked into the bathroom.

So you take an HD shot of the roach, add a note—"OMG!! WTF??!! There's a ginormous ROACH in my room at the XYZ Hotel"—and hit "Send." And then your comments and the photo of the roach are instantly uploaded to your 7,000 Twitter followers and your 3,300 LinkedIn associates and your 587 closest friends on Facebook. And even assuming that only 10 percent of your contacts are online at the moment, that means that more than 1,000 people will know about the cockroach in the hotel within minutes.

Plus, if you're really bothered by the bug, you might even take the time to upload the picture and your thoughts to XYZ Hotel's ratings page on Yelp, TripAdvisor, or your favorite travel review site.

But the XYZ Hotel's problems don't stop there, because many of your friends and contacts will repost your complaint. A bunch of people will "like" your post, and one or two sickos may even pin the picture on their Pinterest cockroach appreciation boards with a comment such as "Check out this magnificent specimen of a German cockroach my friend spotted at the XYZ Hotel."

So less than ten minutes after you spied the roach, thousands and thousands of people know about it and the XYZ Hotel. And if the hotel's sales and marketing staff aren't monitoring the establishment's name on the Web, they are completely unaware that this sort of news is hopscotching around the globe. They do know, however, that the Mandelbaum bar mitzvah just cancelled, NewCoCorp's meeting planner is no longer considering the hotel for the company's annual sales event, and the XYZ Hotel's reservations are dropping off.

A FIRST WORLD PROBLEM, INDEED

Today the power of smartphones and the Internet, combined with the newly democratized control of information, means every single person you and your brand interface with has the potential to reinforce—or redefine—your messaging. Managed properly, this new situation can be both powerful and profitable. Managed poorly, it's a lot scarier than that disgusting bug crawling around in your bathtub.

Take the example of the new pizza parlor employee, code-named @Cella_, who was fired before she had even started her first day of work after she commented about her new job on Twitter. @Cella_ tweeted her disappointment with starting work at Jet's Pizza in Mansfield, Texas, this way: "Ew, I start this f*** a** job tomorrow," followed by seven thumbs down Emojis.

Another Jet's employee saw the Tweet and showed it to franchise owner Robert Waple, who logged in to send @Cellla_ a tweet of his own: "No you don't start that FA job today! I just fired you! Good luck with your no money, no job life!"

Coincidentally, this same thing happened in my office a few months before @Cella_ posted her outburst. One of our employees (let's call her Maria) had asked for a few days off to visit her sick uncle in Puerto Rico. Even though she didn't have any personal time-off days available, our office manager decided that it was a worthwhile reason, and Maria should be given the extra time.

On Thursday, the day Maria was supposed to return, she sent an e-mail explaining that her uncle had passed away and she was going to stay in San Juan for the funeral. Of course we gave her the extension.

Every Friday morning we have an all-office breakfast at which we talk about what's going on in our business and our lives and catch up with everyone we might not see during the busy week. During this breakfast, our office manager told the assembled group what was going on with Maria and suggested that everyone be sensitive to her loss when she returned.

A moment or two later another young woman held up her laptop and showed us the Facebook page of the employee who was supposedly grieving in Puerto Rico. Instead of a picture of her in all black at the funeral or standing with her uncle in happier times, we saw Maria posing on the beach in a green fluorescent bikini with her arms around her boyfriend. The text read, "Hanging with my Boo in the Bahamas. Can't believe I have to go back to work on Monday."

Even though we did not fire her on Facebook, the result was the same for both Maria and @Cellla_. They lost their jobs because of stupid things they posted on the Internet. But the problem doesn't stop with silly online posts. The democratization of the Internet magnifies everyone's statements and misdeeds and causes the most damage to those who've built the biggest reputations. In other words, the bigger you are, the harder you fall thanks to what I call "the trouble with transparency."

THE TROUBLE WITH TRANSPARENCY

On February 5, 2015, the *New York Times* included two stories on the trouble with transparency that few readers probably connected. One article, headlined "With an Apology, Brian Williams Digs Himself Deeper in Copter Tale," was about *NBC Nightly News* anchor Brian Williams's "misremembered" flight on a US military helicopter that was forced down by enemy fire in 2003. The other, headlined "Pascal Lands in Sony's Outbox," was further down the page and chronicled Sony Pictures Entertainment studio chief Amy Pascal's trouble with transparency after her "denigrating remarks about President Obama's presumed preference for black-themed movies" were revealed to the world after a hacker broke into Sony Pictures' server and posted Pascal's e-mails on the Internet.

So what do articles about a disgraced TV news anchor and a resigning top executive at Sony Pictures have in common? Besides their both having top jobs in the media business, and both taking "indefinite leaves of absence" from those jobs, and both being in trouble for saying offensive things, one salient point was most likely overlooked: both offenders were outed and pilloried on the Internet.

The Williams article quoted CNN's *New Day* host Chris Cuomo as saying, "The Internet would 'eat him [Williams] alive.'" In Pascal's case, hackers revealed her private e-mails in which her comments about the president's movie preferences "became fodder for gossip sites, trade publications and mainstream news organizations."

Not that anyone need worry about either Williams's or Pascal's future. The NBC host had a five-year, $10 million contract with the network, and Sony's executive's exit included a four-year guaranteed payout of $30 to $40 million, plus a percentage of the profits on films she produced, as well as millions of dollars for annual office costs. Neither Williams nor Pascal would have to worry about where their next Fifth Avenue pied-à-terre was coming from, and neither should we.

We should all be worrying, however, about the trouble with transparency—that is, how easily their respective misdeeds were reported and repeated across the Internet. Facts and occurrences that would have taken forever to catch fire years ago now become common knowledge overnight. And whether it's Governor Chris Christie seen rooting against his home team in a private sky box, Mitt Romney getting caught on video making snide comments about "the other 47 percent" to a private audience, @Cellla_ bitching about her new job, or Amy Pascal making offensive comments in what she thought was a private conversation, the key protective word of the pre-Internet days, "private," has become irrelevant.

Whether or not Williams, Pascal, or anyone in similar shoes would be found guilty in a court of law no longer matters. Today people are instantly condemned in the court of public opinion. And today's companies, terrified by the effect of such fiascos on stock price and shareholder value, need to step in quickly with defensive moves to protect their businesses. More importantly, they have to preempt these attacks on their brand value with crisis plans put into place long before they're actually needed. After all, the time to install fire extinguishers and make sure they're properly pressurized is not when you first hear the file alarm ringing down the hall.

Whether it's a student posting a picture from a drunken frat party that later shows up in a background check by a prospective employer or an errant tweet or an e-mail intended for a specific recipient but inadvertently sent to "everyone," the effect of today's democratized communications is so fast—and so universal—that our code of behavior has not yet caught up with the consequences. And so stories like Williams's and Pascal's on the front page of the *New York Times* will only become more frequent, more devastating, and farther reaching.

I'm not suggesting that these folks and many others don't deserve to be outed for their mistruths and misdeeds—although I should add that most of us have said inappropriate things when we didn't think anyone was listening. I sincerely do hope that such transparency will ultimately improve the tone and nature of public discourse and behavior. But in the meantime, every CEO, CMO, marketing professional, parent, and person online needs to vigilantly guard his or her professional and personal reputation. Remember that the walls may not have ears (yet), but every person with a smartphone has a recorder, a video camera, and a simple way to publish your behavior online—and put you on trial—in a world where you are not presumed innocent until proven guilty.

Williams tried to say he was sorry, albeit with inelegant, ham-fisted apologies that used tortuous words such as "conflated," "misremembered," and "the fog of memory." But even his clumsy explanations are not the reason why he's finished. After all, we've endured a litany of fat-tongued celebrities' awkward explanations as they grasped for redemption, from Jimmy Swaggart's tears to Larry Craig's "wide stance" to Paula Deen's not understanding the *N*-word to Tammy Faye Bakker's Mascara-Gate.

Williams has promised to get back on the air, saying, "Upon my return I will continue my career-long effort to be worthy of the trust of those who place their trust in us." But it won't happen. Regardless of the time, money, and effort NBC has invested in his career, not to mention his charisma, talent, and good looks, Williams will never regain his gravitas. He might return to television and enjoy a successful career as a humorist or entertainer. But he will not be an anchorman again.

It's not that others haven't lied and then succeeded at winning second chances. Lots of famous people lie to their audiences, suffer temporary setbacks, and come back to enjoy bigger and better public images.

President Bill Clinton did it. His assertion "I did not have sexual relations with that woman" turned out to be a lie. But today he is one of the most beloved political statesmen in the world.

His wife, Hillary Clinton, did it too. She "misstated" coming under sniper fire during a visit to Bosnia in the 1990s and had to admit that those claims weren't true after video footage showed the First Lady walking calmly away from her plane. But now Clinton is a former US senator and secretary of state and, as of this writing, the leading Democratic presidential candidate for 2016.

But Brian Williams is toast.

The key to Bill Clinton's impeachment was not what he said when he covered up his marital misdeeds but his breech of the law when he lied to Congress under oath. And Hillary Clinton's lie (a story coincidentally similar to Williams's) hasn't seemed to derail her ambitions very much either.

So why is Brian Williams toast when so many others have managed to skate around their "misremembering" to little bad effect? It's simple: no one really cares when politicians lie because—sad but true—no one really expects politicians to tell the truth in the first place. But Brian Williams is toast because as a journalist he violated his core value, his defining ideal, and his authentic truth when he lied to himself and to us.

In a violent year when over sixty journalists around the world had died trying to tell the real story, Williams's tale of false bravado stood out as a betrayal of not just the NBC anchor's audience but of all the brave men and women who really were in harm's way. And there's no way *NBC Nightly News*'s 9.3 million viewers would ever forgive that.

Williams stood for the truth, and his career was based on delivering that truth to his viewers. Unfortunately for the newscaster, violating that promise was seen as an unpardonable infidelity. Brian Williams's brand value rested on unflappable trust, and he tarnished it. Trust takes years to build, seconds to break, and forever to repair. And by lying to us, Williams made the biggest mistake of all: he took something abstract and made it personal. Williams took a story that was all about him and made it all about us.

THE LURE OF ASPIRATIONAL PRODUCTS: VICTORIA'S SECRET'S SECRET

In 2014 Victoria's Secret UK showed a lineup of beautiful young women wearing its lingerie under the slogan "The Perfect Body." The ads generated over 26,000 signatures, with angry protesters complaining that the campaign was "offensive and damaging to women." The uproar was not enough to get Victoria's Secret to apologize or scuttle the campaign, but the company did reissue the same ad with a new headline, "A Body for Everybody."

Apparently Victoria's Secret wanted its naysayers to know that the company had heard them and responded appropriately. But in its rush to do as little as possible to rectify the situation, Victoria's Secret used the same picture for the ongoing campaign and continued to use similar images in all of its advertising and marketing. Ironically, Victoria's Secret imposed its new tagline, "A Body for Everybody," over a picture showing only one body type.

It made no sense that "The Perfect Body" was damaging enough for people to protest but the picture of ten tall, thin, young, busty, beautiful women with long straight hair in their underwear was not. After all, if the problem with the tagline was the suggestion that all women need to conform to a particular body type to be perfect and beautiful, why didn't the photo cause the same uproar?

The bigger question really has to do with whom Victoria's Secret's advertising targets in the first place and what that audience responds to.

For years, advertising for men's clothing was created to appeal to women because the reigning wisdom was that women bought 80 percent of men's clothes for their husbands, sons, boyfriends, and so forth. While this purchase percentage has changed somewhat in the last few years, the belief that women buy, or are responsible for motivating the purchase of, most menswear is still fairly universal.

But women's wear is different. Not only do men not buy very much of it for the women in their lives (not even the sexy lingerie Victoria's Secret sells), but most women don't even dress for men; instead they dress for themselves and for other women.

This suggests that Victoria's Secret used homogenized sexy images not to satisfy a male view of what men want the women in their lives to look like but to appeal to the very women who buy Victoria's Secret's products in the first place—few of whom probably look like the models in the ads. Instead, Victoria's Secret is presenting an aspirational view of how the women who buy their products want to look.

Of course this practice is not limited to female shoppers. Regardless of whether men or women buy Tommy Bahama men's clothes, it's interesting to note that Andy Lucchesi, the model used in the ads for the past decade, can't be much more than forty-years-old but sports the gray hair of someone at least half again as old. Tommy Bahama's message, just like Victoria's Secret's, is simple: you are younger, better looking, and in better shape than your age (or actual condition) would suggest, and wearing our clothes will only enhance that impression.

And before you think that only clothing manufacturers use this strategy to sell their products to insecure consumers, understand that it's not only fashion that uses the aspirational strategy. Plenty of products sell not for what they do but for what their purchasers envision them doing.

THE CARS WE BUY VERSUS THE WAY WE DRIVE

Sports cars such as Porsches and Ferraris, for example, are designed to drive 180 miles per hour on the German Autobahn. Why then is the manufacturers' biggest market in the United States, a country where the national average speed limit is generally between fifty-five and seventy miles per hour? What's more, while there might be open roads in the western and southwestern regions of the country, where these cars could actually reach their intended speeds, the majority of these performance marvels are driven in urban areas where speeds are controlled not just by legal limits but by such practical considerations as traffic and congestion.

In 2010 TomTom, the Dutch company that produces navigation and mapping products, released its study of domestic American driving speeds, based on data collected by its devices in the Speed Profiles Program. The company discovered that despite the capability of today's cars, few Americans actually drive much faster than allowed.

AutoBlog reported on it this way:

> The two years of data collection shows that, overall, Americans tend to drive within the acceptable limits of the law overall, but the average speed of your journey will typically be determined by where you're driving.
>
> . . . Mississippi has the fastest roads on average, with typical speeds at just over 70 miles per hour, followed by New Mexico. The fastest single interstate is I-15 in Utah and Nevada, with speeds averaging 77.67 mph. . . . The biggest speed winners are in the middle of the country: Mississippi, Nebraska, Kansas, Iowa, Idaho, Alabama and Missouri all exceed an average of 67 mph.

Clearly then, people are buying cars such as Chevrolet Corvettes and BMW M4s for reasons other than their high performance and top speeds.

And it's not just that sports cars are selling to people who do not plan to drive them as their designers intended. Few four-wheel drive sports-utility vehicles ever go off road or do anything an old-fashioned station wagon couldn't do just as well. But they are still promoted and sold in ways that feature their four-wheel drive systems and off-road capability. While some of these vehicles may be used in icy, snowy winter conditions or on unpaved roads or even on off-road excursions, that still does not explain why thousands of off-road vehicles are sold in sunbelt cities and areas where there is no need for their out-sized capabilities.

A 1996 survey conducted by J. D. Power and Associates found that "56% of all sport-utility vehicles never even leave the pavement and only 5% go off-road with any regularity." And while Jeep claims that 60 percent of Wrangler owners do go off road, the industry average is considered to be less than 10 percent.

What companies are selling and consumers are buying is not the actual ability to drive at triple-digit speeds or across mountains and deserts but the aspiration to do so. Driving these overly capable vehicles is more about the image they bestow on their drivers than what they actually accomplish. In other words, you don't have to actually do these things; it's just good to know that you could.

Before you laugh at your neighbor with the expensive Jaguar or Land Rover, realize these aspirational purchases are not limited to cars and trucks: our Olympics-quality running shoes don't help us run any faster, our state-of-the-art laptops don't make our prose any more profound, our ceramic chefs' knives don't cut our frozen pizzas any straighter, and our Eric Clapton limited-edition vintage Fender Stratocaster electric guitars don't give our blues riffs any more feeling. Not only is product competence cost-of-entry, but—as we've seen—most consumers don't actually use all of the functional bene-fits of their purchases in the first place.

Instead, we use these products to help assuage the discom-fort brought on by our modern existence and by the specific myths that keep us from accomplishing our goals. Specifically, they are the myth of uniqueness and the myth of competency.

BE UNIQUE . . . JUST LIKE EVERYONE ELSE

The Myth of Uniqueness

Remember American cowboy movies? The hero rolled into town and almost immediately confronted the bad guys and bullies who had made frontier life nearly unbearable. Of course, despite the sheriff and his deputies and all the other cowboys with guns, our hero was the only one who could overcome insurmountable odds to drive out the bad guys and save the charming little town with nothing more than his trusty horse and a six-shooter. And he was unique—the only one who could do what needed to be done.

But when our hero was done mopping up the bad guys, what did he do? Did he help the town create a wastewater committee and build a sewage treatment facility to provide a sustainable water reclamation protocol for the future? Did he work with the one-room schoolhouse's PTA to improve literacy for fifth graders? Did he start a charitable fund to buy leg braces for bowlegged cowboys? No, our one-of-a-kind hero rode off into the sunset. Alone.

For those of us raised on a steady diet of Western culture, the spirit of the unique individual lives on. We are bombarded with images that romanticize the silent, stoic hero, from the Marlboro Man to Batman, from John Wayne to Bruce Wayne. We have all been seduced by the lure of uniqueness.

Everywhere you turn people laud uniqueness: "No two snowflakes are alike," they tell you. "No two fingerprints are the same." These platitudes make being unique sound simple and easy. But do you know what "unique" actually means? The dictionary definition is "being the only one." Unless you add a modifier such as "fairly," as in "fairly unique," the word is absolute—it leaves no room for compromise. You either are the only one or you're not. You can't be a little unique anymore than you can be a little excellent, a little perfect, or a little pregnant. Either you're unique or you're not.

Think about how few successful people actually pass the strict definition of "unique." We all stand on the shoulders of giants, and even the most successful people have built their success on what came before.

But being noticed does not require uniqueness in the fingerprint or snowflake category. Instead it requires you to be fairly differentiated so that your audience can recognize and respect your differences.

Before you think I'm giving you a pass on the nearly impossible task of defining your uniqueness, know this: success doesn't usually come to the truly unique because their audiences don't understand what they're offering in the first place.

History is riddled with stories of the unique who were ignored and denied until an act of fate mainstreamed them. Joan of Arc? Burned at the stake. Van Gogh? Committed suicide. Jimi Hendrix? Died of an overdose. Forging a truly unique path is not the way to success or happiness. And, of course, there are also the many unfortunate unique characters who never got their break and labored in obscurity. Even the businessman of the century, Steve Jobs, was fired by Apple years before he made his stunning comeback and turned Apple into the largest and most profitable company in the world.

The Myth of Competency

If you spend a lot of time on the Internet and read a lot of the teachings of the new gurus of prosperity and productivity, you'll encounter a great deal of advice that tells you to "be the best" or "be sensational." That seemingly good advice becomes the insurmountable obstacle that often helps create our First World problems and stands in the way of accomplishment.

If competency were the only quality required for success, then your talented friend who moved to Hollywood to be a movie star or your niece who moved to New York to perform on Broadway would already be a big success. The truth is, the most talented people very often don't make it to the top. They're too concerned about being great to get there.

Think about that wonderful guitar player you know. You brag to all your friends that he's just as good as Jimmy Page, just as good as Jeff Beck. And maybe he is. But if he sits in his room practicing his arpeggios all day every day, no one will ever get to hear how well he plays.

Success actually requires more than virtuosity. It calls for perseverance, marketing, attention to detail, and more than a little luck. But if you're too busy sitting home, writing and rewriting your prose or obsessively perfecting your sales pitch, you'll never get the chance to get out there and make something happen.

2

ALL ABOUT THEM
IN THE DIGITAL WORLD

LIFE'S GREAT MYSTERY

One of life's great mysteries is how the boy who wasn't good enough to marry your daughter can be the father of the smartest grandchild in the world.

THOSE WHO CAN'T DO, TEACH

After waiting behind the curtain during the interminable introduction, the speaker slowly walked to the front of the stage where he was greeted with tepid applause. He was wearing his typical uniform of navy blue polo shirt, baggy rumpled khakis, and Converse Jack Taylor All-Star sneakers—without laces. The single punctuation for his outfit was his owlish glasses, this time lighting up his face with a bright fuchsia neon color.

The speaker stared quietly at the crowd of 2,000 for a few seconds. He cleared his throat, opened his mouth, and said softly but firmly, "Those who can't do . . . teach."

The audience was shocked. Some shifted uncomfortably in their seats and grumbled their disapproval. Some considered storming out in a huff but quickly thought better of it. Instead they glanced around the room, looking at each other for confirmation of what they had just heard while they waited for him to continue.

The speaker was addressing a national convention of teachers!

Over the next forty-five minutes or so, the speaker told the audience why he believed teaching to be the most important job in the world. He explained that practitioners do what they're good at because they've trained to do it their entire lives. Attorneys litigate, surgeons operate, accountants keep books, and mechanics repair cars—that's what they are trained to do. And when they do their jobs, they can help one or two people at a time.

But, he continued, only the finest practitioners are actually qualified to teach. And when they do, they help more than just the people in their classrooms. They actually improve the lives of all the people their students will go on to help throughout their careers. By paying it forward, teachers magnify their knowledge hundreds and possibly thousands of times over.

Teaching, the speaker went on to explain, is not just a job, not just a career, but one of the most important undertakings to which a person can devote his or her life. Teaching, he concluded, is the most sacred and meaningful way to make one's life matter long after one is gone. "Teaching is not just a vocation," he concluded, "it's a legacy."

Done making his point, the speaker paused for a moment before he walked to the very front of the stage where he began his talk forty-five minutes before. He stared wordlessly at the crowd again, took a deep breath, and repeated, "Those who can't do, teach."

They were the same five words he had opened his presentation with—the same five words that had shocked and angered his audience. But this time the crowd heard the speaker's words in a whole new way. And instead of staring noiselessly back at the speaker, the audience members leapt to their feet in a raucous standing ovation that seemed to go on forever.

WITH ALL DUE RESPECT

We've all heard the insults. Chances are we've probably repeated them at some time or another too.

Maybe we said, "Those who can't do, teach," when discussing someone's qualifications for his or her job.

Perhaps we were at a Christmas party and asked an attorney if she'd evicted all her widows and orphans before New Year's Eve.

Maybe we muttered something about a policeman eating donuts or a fireman sitting on his keister in the firehouse all day long.

Regardless of the insult, how the hearer heard it made it more poignant than what we actually meant.

Which is why the speaker at the national convention was able to turn around an entire room of teachers simply by redefining a sentence they had heard all their lives and which they had previously interpreted as a biting insult.

By turning that insult on its head, the speaker managed not only to neuter and defang it but to transform it into a source of inspiration. By removing the hurt and replacing it with pride, he almost instantly changed how the teachers gathered in that room felt about him, yes, but more importantly, how they felt about themselves and their chosen career.

The speaker took an insult that had belittled teachers for years and turned it into a point of pride. He didn't just compliment the audience members or make them feel good about themselves; he turned a liability into an asset. And by turning a weakness into a strength, he also transformed his listeners, giving them a greater feeling of power and confidence.

The speaker understood that making people feel good about themselves is a quick way to make them feel good about what you have to say. That's what All About Them is all about.

WHY DOPAMINE IS YOUR FRIEND

But it's not just empathetic speakers who can create good feelings in others to help get their ideas across and demonstrate value. In today's increasingly technological world, digital devices are also creating positive outcomes by generating positive feelings.

Studies show that each time our smartphones, digital tablets, and laptops "ping" us with the promise of an incoming message, our brains release a stimulating shot of dopamine. Over time, reacting to this self-inflicted joy juice becomes a training protocol that teaches us to respond to attention. And just as Pavlov's dogs learned to salivate when they heard the peal of the dinner bell, we also respond each and every time our phones summon us to pay attention. And we do so regardless of the priority of the message they are alerting us to.

The psychological impact of our devices is so powerful that Peter Whybrow, director of the Semel Institute for Neuroscience and Human Behavior at the University of California, Los Angeles, says, "The computer is like electronic cocaine," creating waves of depression and mania in its users.

Magazines from the *Atlantic* to *Newsweek* have published extensively about the connection between dopamine addictions and the compulsion today's consumers feel about using smartphones and other Internet-enabled devices.

Newsweek says, "The average person, regardless of age, sends or receives about 400 texts a month, four times the 2007 number. The average teen processes an astounding 3,700 texts a month, double the 2007 figure. And more than two-thirds of these normal, everyday cyborgs, (the author included), report feeling their phone vibrate when in fact nothing is happening."

Imagine: in less than twenty years, a behavior once considered unusual and even freakish is now not only accepted but embraced by virtually every consumer in the First World and by every person reading this book.

But here's where the fast pace of evolution becomes even more interesting: when we look at technological advances, we find progress increases exponentially. In fact, Moore's law, which states that the number of transistors in an integrated circuit doubles every two years, is not just a literal measurement but a metaphorical one as well. Not only does the number of transistors in a circuit double, but so do the circuits' speed, power, and capability. And while they're getting faster and stronger, these transistors are completely changing the way we interact with the environment and each other.

But here's the great irony: at the same time that transistors are following their inexorable path to increased capacity and speed, the processing power of the operator of the circuit and the device it is installed in adapts at a much slower evolutionary pace. In the case of us humans, history shows it takes a few hundred thousand years to develop a species-wide reaction to certain stimuli. Think about it. Each new release of your favorite software seems to double the speed of whatever that software does for you. At this point, the software is speeding up so much that the results are hardly even noticeable. But our ability to utilize the faster and faster applications can't possibly keep pace.

Of course it wasn't always this way. Before the computerized technological upheaval we're all experiencing today, machines were sometimes designed to actually slow their interaction with humans. An example is the modern keyboard.

Have you ever wondered why the typical computer keyboard is laid out the way it is? Wouldn't it be easier to learn if the keys had been arranged in alphabetical order or some other more efficient manner? In 1873, when keyboards were first designed to be used on typewriters (not computers!), an intentionally inefficient layout—called QWERTY because of the first six letters found on the top row—was created to keep the keys from jamming. To do this, some of the most used keys, such as those for *A* and *S* and *L*, were placed where they would be most slowly activated by a human typist's weaker fingers. In fact, while 70 percent of English words can be typed with the letters *A*, *D*, *E*, *H*, *I*, *N*, *O*, *P*, *S*, and *T*, only

four of those ten letters are placed on the typewriter's second—or home—row, where they would be most accessible.
What's more, while only about 300 English words can be
typed on a standard QWERTY keyboard with the right hand
alone, over 3,000 words can be type by the left hand. While
QWERTY does favor left-handed typists, this only helps an
estimated 5 to 30 percent of the world's population, leaving
some 70 to 95 percent of right-handed people to type with
their weaker hand.

Today, however, technology is developing so much faster
than our capacity to adapt that fewer and fewer allowances are
made for our inabilities. Instead, that difference—specifically,
the breakneck speed at which digital capabilities increase versus the evolutionary pace at which human abilities advance—is
an ever-increasing chasm that defines the new world we all
live in.

The enormous changes digital devices have wrought in our
social activity since their introduction have happened almost
without our knowledge or understanding. Coupled with the
different speeds of growth, this finds us diving headlong into a
brave new world where we're bombarded by constant stimuli
we don't understand, don't know how to interpret, and won't
evolve to manage properly for thousands of years.

In 1936 Albert Einstein published an essay titled "Self-
Portrait," in which he wrote, "Of what is significant in one's
own existence one is hardly aware, and it certainly should
not bother the other fellow. What does a fish know about
the water in which he swims all his life?" Einstein's words
provide the perfect interpretation of the situation we find
ourselves in today.

Years from now historians will look back at these days with the benefit of hindsight and be able to interpret them properly for posterity. But while we're living them, it's difficult to actually see the ultimate impact of what's going on all around us. We do know, however, that the digital revolution we are experiencing is profoundly changing the way we function, the way we think, and the way we behave.

"WE HAVE MET THE ENEMY AND HE IS US": POGO THE POSSUM

Pat your pocket, look in your purse, or scan your desktop. I'll bet you've got your smartphone or Internet-enabled tablet close at hand right now. There's even a good chance that you're reading this book on your digital device.

According to the *Daily Mail*'s survey of over 2,000 smartphone owners, "The average user now picks up their device more than 1,500 times a week."

Average users reach for their phones at 7:31 a.m. in the morning and check personal e-mails and Facebook before they even get out of bed. Average owners use their phones for three hours and sixteen minutes a day. Almost four in ten admitted to feeling lost without their device.

Can you guess how many smartphones and connected tablets there are in the world today? As of March 2015 there were 7 billion. Believe it or not, that means more people in the world own these devices than own toothbrushes. And the trend shows no sign of slowing: estimates are that sales will triple by 2019. That will mean over 21 billion connected devices around the world.

Of course, with all these connected gizmos, people can't just be using their devices to talk to their friends. They are also doing business and shopping. According to IBM Retail Analytics as reported on CNBC, retail sales made on mobile devices increased 27 percent in 2014 to make up 22 percent of all online sales.

Our gadgets are doing so much business, as reported by the *Harvard Business Review*, that "the research firm Forrester estimates that e-commerce is now approaching $200 billion in revenue in the United States alone and accounts for 9% of total retail sales, up from 5% five years ago." And it's not just in the United States. "The corresponding figure is about 10% in the United Kingdom, 3% in Asia-Pacific, and 2% in Latin America."

Smartphones and tablets have also become the media of the future. While some might prefer their traditional newspapers, televisions, radios, and desktop computers, the smartphone is the only device that people carry with them all the time. And they refer to them constantly.

John Lennon's saying "Life is what happens while you're busy making other plans" presciently foreshadowed the strange new world we each find ourselves in. And whether or not we are willing participants in this technological upheaval, the world around us is changing at an ever-increasing—and ever-confounding—speed.

Most interestingly, despite the increased connections the new digital technology makes possible, many people find themselves more and more isolated. That is because the interaction with our smartphones and tablets takes precedence over the people sending us the messages.

Imagine you and I are having a conversation. Midway through our talk I excuse myself to answer a call from my wife. That would suggest that I've prioritized talking to my wife over continuing my conversation with you. But later on that evening I could be having a face-to-face conversation with my wife at home when you phoned, and I'd interrupt my chat with my wife to answer your call. My earlier logic would suggest that now I'm prioritizing my conversation with you over my conversation with my wife. Yet that wouldn't be true. Instead the siren call of the device, not any specific person, takes precedence in either scenario. We care more about the phone alerting us to the person *we could be talking to* than about talking to the person we're actually having a conversation with.

Because of this Pavlovian response—causing us to metaphorically salivate when the bell rings—marketers who use digital interruption technologies (e-mails, texts, phone calls) to reach their prospects have learned to increase the number of interactions and distribute them across many different media. And even though most of us wonder aloud "Who would ever buy anything based on a cold call or spam e-mail," the odds of success are high enough—and the cost of entry low enough—that those practices continue. At its most basic, *consumer face time*—the amount of time a brand has to interact with a prospect—is critically important and becomes even more valuable when that time is initiated with a shot of dopamine and used to make the prospect feel good.

For years, Verizon Wireless ran an ad for its cell phone service with the tagline "Can you hear me now?" In the campaign, actor Paul Marcarelli, otherwise known as "the Verizon Guy," wandered across the country and across the TV screen repeating, "Can you hear me now?" into his cellphone. Of course he was aping the question most of us ask when our cell service cuts in and out, suggesting Verizon's network is so robust that its subscribers enjoy better connections and fewer disconnects than users of any other service.

But the campaign was successfully intrusive for a more strategic reason: the obvious implication was that Verizon customers could spend more time on their devices and would therefore have better and stronger relationships because of these longer conversations. Sure, we could ask the question "Can you hear me now?" of people with faulty cell phone connections, but we could also ask it of people to whom we are trying to make a point.

This suggests that Verizon was claiming not just that it provided better cell phone connections but that those very connections would help facilitate something we all long for: to be understood. According to Verizon, its services could almost ensure that children would listen to their mothers, husbands and wives would listen to each other, and bosses and employees would communicate better too. "Can you hear me now?" assured consumers not only of improved technical transmission of their calls but also of enhanced basic communication. "Can you hear me now?" responded to both the practical need and the existential desire.

"Can you hear me now?" was an All About Them statement. It perfectly transmits the power of All About Them because ultimately it wasn't about the company that pitched it but the consumer who heard it. "Can you hear me now?" was such a successful campaign, by the way, that while Marcarelli had already appeared in numerous commercials for Dasani,

Heineken, Merrill Lynch, and Old Navy, his professional recognition with Verizon was so strong that *Entertainment Weekly*
named him one of its most intriguing people of 2002. And
this for mouthing what we might otherwise consider an annoyance: an advertising tagline.

THE AGE OF TRANSPARENCY

Not only has the emergence of digital technology meant that
we are all reachable 24/7/365 and eager to communicate
across that time frame, but the information that we share is
always available for review and rebuke.

In the old days (read: before the Internet) data was stored in
libraries and archives, available to those willing to search for it
but not instantly recallable or replicable.

Specific television programs, for example, were aired once
or twice in a season and might sporadically resurface in reruns
but were otherwise unobtainable. Newspaper and magazine articles could be tracked down but required painstaking combing
through stored back issues and grainy microfiche. Even politicians were free to say almost anything they wanted because
it was extremely difficult for anyone to find unimpeachable
documentation of their utterances weeks, months, and years
after their speeches.

Compare that to the searchable sea of data we have access
to today.

Organizations such as the Google Books Library Project
have committed themselves to scanning and digitizing all of
mankind's written works. Since Google Books' founding in
2004, it has digitized and cataloged over 30 million volumes,

an undertaking the University of Michigan hails as "unprecedented access to what may become the largest online body of human knowledge" and author Malte Herwig calls "the democratization of knowledge."

Companies such as Netflix and Amazon have done the same with television and movies, making most of the footage released over the last fifty years available with the click of a mouse. From foreign films to small independent releases to 1960s sitcoms, today's viewer has access to a staggering amount of on-screen entertainment and information that was never available before. And today's enormous collection of information requires almost no effort to retrieve, just an Internet connection, a subscription to each company's library, and a web-enabled digital device—and most of us carry one of these around in our pockets everyday without thinking twice about it or the access it provides.

Newscaster Brian Williams's deception cost him his job because he violated his authentic truth and told a story about being shot down in wartime that turned out to be a lie. Particularly interesting about his unfortunate situation is how quickly and easily it arose thanks to the availability of digital data, which made uncovering his fraud so easy. What's more, disgusted viewers' ability to vent their anger across social media platforms like Facebook and Twitter sped up his very rapid demise: to minimize the damage Williams could cause the company's core brand, NBC quickly removed him from its roster. Of course others besides Williams have paid the price levied by retrievable media and almost instantaneous criticism. And these new phenomena have not only ended careers but also created them.

Jon Stewart's groundbreaking *The Daily Show* was able to provide biting satirical commentary because it could document public figures' hypocrisy with actual footage of their deceptions. For example, Stewart's research staff found a clip in which Fox News anchor Sean Hannity had doctored Congresswoman Michele Bachmann's anti-health-care reform rally. Stewart also showed CNBC financial show host Jim Kramer promising, "Your money is safe in Bear Stearns," just six days before the firm folded. And the show built its reputation and viewership by airing back-to-back video footage of a wide array of hapless politicians repeatedly contradicting themselves in different speeches delivered to different audiences.

In the past, these video clips would have surfaced only after armies of interns had waded through hours and hours of footage. But SnapStream, a video production company in Texas, has developed an application that records television programs directly on a computer's hard drive and then makes keyword searches possible—in much the same way that YouTube provides access to consumer-generated videos.

Besides the app's capability to record and research footage, the key to SnapStream's technological advance is the program's ability to search the footage's closed-captioning systems with a text-based search system. That way researchers can find what they need quickly and easily. It is such an effective system that in 2014, the *Wrap* reported that *Daily Show* senior producer Pat King estimated SnapStream had cut the staff's workload by 60 to 70 percent! "It used to take 10 or 12 minutes to get a clip into an Avid editor," said King. "Now it's much faster, which makes for a smoother process from writing to rewrites to rehearsal and air."

Imagine what will happen when all the footage the various cable and technology networks make available has been scanned for instantaneous search. Suddenly every public utterance will be available for discussion and dissection and immediately uploadable to social media sites like Twitter, Facebook, and whatever comes next. All of a sudden, viewers and consumers will have the power to act as judge, jury, and executioner, decide instantly what is true and what isn't, and immediately share their opinions—and the corresponding evidence—with the rest of the world.

But despite the rapid development of these video retrieval technologies, we don't have to wait until all recorded speech becomes instantly reviewable to experience the power of transparency. Online rating systems have become so powerful and influential that businesses, from restaurants to car dealerships to public speakers to surgeons, are all feeling the effects.

Websites such as Yelp, eBay, TripAdvisor, and Amazon have all embraced consumer-generated review technology, inviting satisfied and unhappy users alike to post their comments for everyone to see. Given the broad reach of social media sites and the almost instant retrieval of search engines, these rating systems have the power to make or break a business instantly and almost effortlessly.

Professionals, too, are feeling the effects of this ubiquitous new rating technology. Sites like Angie's List and HomeAdvisor review handymen; WebMD and RateMD grade physicians; and Avvo.com and Lawyers.com review attorneys. Today's consumers can arm themselves with unprecedented amounts of data on their intended service providers before they ever make a purchase or hiring decision.

Unfortunately, all this information does not necessarily make smarter consumers; nor does it ensure better services. According to *USA Today*, "Doing what's best for patients won't necessarily make them happy."

As Adam and Eve learned on their exile from the Garden of Eden, knowledge does not necessarily lead to happiness. And while review sites may empower consumers to know more about the restaurants they dine in and the doctors they visit, the sites may also be negatively affecting the products and services consumers are getting.

In the laboratory, scientific researchers who plan investigative studies must always account for a phenomenon known as the "observer effect." Simply put, the observer effect states that the mere act of observation can actually change that which is being observed. For example, a regulation thermometer must either capture or surrender thermal energy to record a temperature, and in doing so, it actually changes the temperature of whatever it is evaluating.

Besides all that, it's important to remember that facts and figures and surveys and studies can be manipulated to support almost any outcome a marketer is looking to promote.

Consider the following quote from the September 2015 issue of *Men's Journal*: "In a new Danish study, recreational runners who ran 10 miles per hour versus a slow jog of five miles per hour put 80 percent less stress on their knees." As a runner who's had knee problems, this article seemed insightful and made me rethink my running. But that was only until I looked at it with a more jaundiced eye. While the basic premise is that running faster may be better for your knees, there's no further information on why the studied runners were performing at a faster pace.

In a perfect experiment both the faster and slower runners would have exactly the same physical attributes so the test results could be isolated to just the effects of speed and stride. But of course that's not likely what happened.

Instead the slower runners were probably slower because they were older, heavier, or simply not as gifted as their quicker peers. And so the reasons for their increased knee pain might have more to do with their physical condition or previous injuries or weight than their ultimate speed.

I'm a slow runner and tend to run in the back of my pack, and I'm sure a few of the reasons are that I'm just a donut or two shy of 190 pounds and my years of youthful indiscretions are long behind me. My left knee aches because of an unfortunate skiing accident when I was a reckless nineteen-year-old, and I've come to accept that running faster is neither possible nor a panacea for what ails me.

Whether we're trying to run faster, reviewing politicians' speeches, deciding what restaurant to visit, or picking a vacation spot, more information does not necessarily equal more accurate information. And even though we have access to more and more empirical data, that access does not always result in better decisions.

The two questions we're left with as consumers, then, are how to evaluate the veracity and quality of the coming tsunami of data—a particularly timely problem otherwise known as "infobesity"—and how to make the best possible decisions using all of the tools to which we now have access.

As marketers, we have questions that are at once similar and different. First, how do we manage the waves of increasingly accessible data available about us and our companies? Second, how do we use what we know about this information to help consumers make the best decisions and engage with our companies in order to buy our products or services?

These are the questions that *All About Them* seeks to answer.

3

THE DIFFERENCE BETWEEN CONTENT AND CONTEXT

THE CENSUS TAKER

The census taker knocked twice before anyone responded. Finally an elderly man with a gray beard opened the door.

"Excuse me," said the census taker. "Does Mr. Aaron Goldstein live here?"

"No," answered the old man.

"What's your name?" asked the census taker.

"Aaron Goldstein," the old man replied.

"I thought you said Aaron Goldstein doesn't live here," said the startled census taker.

The old man looked around. "You call this living?"

THE MEANING OF MEANING

In his breakthrough 1996 book *Being Digital*, MIT Media Lab founder Nicholas Negroponte coined the now famous phrase "Content is king." Negroponte contended that with the distribution of data becoming both instantaneous and ubiquitous, the way it moves around is irrelevant but the specific data (measured in bits) that moves around is critical and valuable. According to Negroponte,

> The valuation of a bit is determined in large part by its ability to be used over and over again. In this regard, a Mickey Mouse bit is probably worth a lot more than a Forrest Gump bit, Mickey's bits even come in lollipops (consumable atoms). More interestingly, Disney's guaranteed audience is refueled at a rate that exceeds 12,500 births each hour. In 1994 [back when Negroponte wrote his classic] the market value of Disney was $2 billion greater than that of Bell Atlantic, in spite of Bell Atlantic's sales being 50 percent greater and profits being double.

In a world where content can be created and duplicated with the click of a mouse, content has given way to a more powerful notion. Today, context is king. This mostly unrecognized paradigm shift has been repeated throughout recent history and presents an easy-to-follow road map as you look to put the All About Them idea to work.

Pablo Picasso's *Bull's Head*, for example, presents a hidden-in-plain-sight explanation of the difference between content and context. Picasso created the found-object sculpture in

1942 from the seat and handlebars of a junked bicycle. The artwork has been described as Picasso's most famous creation, a simple yet astonishingly complete metamorphosis. But if one doesn't understand the context in which *Bull's Head* was created, it loses its power to both amaze and instruct.

Today Picasso's construct can be seen as a clever assembly of items, an artistic sleight of hand where two common objects exchange their functional identity for a visual identity and create something new. Hence, handlebars and bicycle seat become a bull's head.

But a deeper dive into the context of Picasso's sculpture says something all together different. After the turn of the century, his country, Spain, underwent three horrific phenomena that changed the entire tenor of Spanish culture forever. Picasso's sculpture is our unlikely tour guide to the significance of those times.

When we look through the bloodied lens of the era in which Picasso worked, we see that the artist was making a statement about the metamorphosis not of the items he assembled but of his home country.

The 1918 influenza pandemic, known as the Spanish flu, infected over 500 million people around the globe. By the time it ran its course, the disease had killed an estimated 50 to 100 million people worldwide, or approximately 3 percent of the global population—significantly more than all the people who died in World War I. The flu was so virulent that it killed more people in its first year than the bubonic plague, known to history as the Black Death, did in the four years from 1347 to 1351. Before the 1918 influenza pandemic was over, more than 8 million Spaniards had succumbed.

Less than one generation after that tragedy, a violent civil war erupted in Spain in 1936. By the time Generalissimo Francisco Franco declared victory three years later, an estimated 200,000 to 300,000 Spaniards had lost their lives.

But the end of the civil war did not mean an end to the glut of Spanish deaths. Under the ultranationalist generalissimo's iron fist, the fascist government built more than 190 concentration camps throughout the country. An estimated 200,000 to 400,000 of Franco's political and ideological enemies died in those camps through forced labor or execution.

Before this string of horrific incidents, Spain was a largely pastoral country. Thanks to the imposing Pyrenees mountain range that isolated the country from its neighbors to the north, Spain had more in common with its southern African neighbors than with France and the rest of Europe. From the 700s until Christopher Columbus sailed to America in 1492, Spain's dominant culture was Muslim, not Christian. And after the economic hardship experienced once Spain's heady romance with New World gold came to an abrupt end, the country effectively sealed itself off from the rest of the continent. This separation was so complete that Spain was said to be in Europe but not of Europe. Further, Franco's fascist government did nothing to improve the country's relationship with the outside world. Thanks to these self-imposed limitations, Spanish culture evolved very differently from the rest of Europe's.

For generations the symbol of Picasso's country of origin was the bull, *el toro*. This noble beast represented power, transportation, food, valor, machismo—an impressively complete inventory of all of the symbolic attributes of the Spanish people.

But as we've seen, the gruesome events of the twentieth century did much to change the tenor of the country.

Picasso's statement, then, created in the relative safety of France and assembled from collected junk, was not about the simple coincidence of the two items' forming a bull's head; rather the artist was commenting on the transformation Spain had undergone. In Picasso's view, what was once agrarian was now industrial. What was once organic had been modified by the hand of man. What was once natural had become mechanized. And a society that had once been lovingly created from centuries of nurturing and development was now brutally crafted from junk.

And so, while the sculpture's content carried little value, its context conveyed the devastation of almost 9 million lives lost as well as the rich culture and human potential buried alongside them.

A few years later, this time in the United States, Andy Warhol created his 1962 *Campbell's Soup Can* paintings. Like Picasso's bull's head, this series also yields a particularly telling insight into the desires and motivations of an entire generation—in this case American workingwomen.

History tells us that Warhol was inspired by Roy Lichtenstein's pulp comic paintings and interested in the idea of transforming highly recognizable images into art. And so the artist purchased a stack of Campbell's soup cans, projected them onto canvas, and traced their images with mechanical precision.

While the initial series did create a mild stir when exhibited at the Ferus Gallery in Los Angeles, most of the public dismissed Warhol's work as junk. But again, a lack of understanding of the context in which he created the *Campbell's Soup Can* series neuters its power to inform.

Like Picasso, Warhol was working in a country and culture vastly changed by the seismic events of the twentieth century: post–World War II America.

During the war, 16.1 million American men had served in the military for an average enlistment of thirty-three months. A full three-quarters served overseas and were out of the country for an average of sixteen months. And sadly, 291,557 of them never returned at all.

During wartime the tenor of the nation changed drastically. With so many men away in the service, women moved from their traditional roles in the home to positions in business and industry. Rosie the Riveter, a fictional can-do worker with her sleeve rolled up over a bulging bicep and a red-and-white polka-dotted scarf tied around her head, probably best represented this "new woman."

Over 19 million American women worked outside the home during World War II. And while many of them may have already been working to help support themselves or their families before the war, during wartime they moved into the manufacturing and executive positions customarily occupied by men—the very men who had crossed the Atlantic or Pacific Ocean to help the war effort. Of course these newly working women were expected to return to their traditional roles after the war ended—but they didn't.

A generation earlier, during World War I, the pop hit "How Ya Gonna Keep 'Em Down on the Farm (After They've Seen Paree)?" dealt with the problem of getting servicemen who had been drafted from rural locales in the southern and midwestern United States to return home to their less sophisticated homes after they'd served overseas in Europe.

As the song's Mr. Reuben asks his wife,

> How ya gonna keep 'em down on the farm
> After they've seen Paree?
> How ya gonna keep 'em away from Broadway
> Jazzin' around and paintin' the town?
> How ya gonna keep 'em away from harm, that's a mystery
> They'll never want to see a rake or plow.
> And who the deuce can parleyvous a cow?
> How ya gonna keep 'em down on the farm
> After they've seen Paree?

But after World War II the problem was different. How could society expect women who had tasted professional success to give it all up and return to their previously subservient roles once their fathers, sons, husbands, and brothers had returned from their overseas war duty?

And so Warhol's pop art paintings, ostensibly just simple reproductions of common soup cans, take on a whole new meaning when seen in this light.

In earlier days when a woman's traditional place was believed to be in the home, cooking was an art. Most meals were made from scratch and were the result of time, knowledge, skill, craftsmanship, creativity, and, yes, love. But now that a significant number of women were working outside the home and had less time to create meals, the art of cooking had become mechanized. And so, if food had been art, thanks to societal changes and Warhol's interpretation, art was now food. And now the food was mechanized, mass-produced, and canned.

Understanding the contemporary context in which Warhol operated gives us a whole different way of looking at both his work and his societal situation. And looking at Warhol's art with a knowledge of that context provides us with a deeper understanding of what was going on at the time and how such cataclysmic changes were about to transform the country and the world.

But perhaps these examples feel a little dated and hard to relate to your day-to-day life. In that case, let's zoom to the twenty-first century and take a look at the contextual statements of a contemporary artist.

PAY NO ATTENTION TO THE MAN BEHIND THE CURTAIN

When I was a boy growing up in Miami Beach, we had a black-and-white television. When my brother and sister and I would whine to our father that we wanted a color set, he'd shrug and patiently explain that we couldn't get color TV because we only had black-and-white electricity. Worse, my mother would add that we would get a color TV when the world turned black and white. Apparently we three kids were very gullible because when I left for college, I had still only watched color TV at my friends' houses.

So there I was during my freshman year of college, sitting with my new friends in the dorm watching one of my favorite movies, *The Wizard of Oz*. Of course you've seen the classic MGM movie. It starts with Dorothy in Kansas, and because it's an old movie, it's in black and white. But suddenly the tornado picks up Dorothy's house and spins her off to Munchkinland, and when she lands (smack dab on top of the Wicked Witch of the East's head, of course), the movie erupts in glorious Technicolor, with the Wicked Witch's brilliant ruby slippers sticking out from under the house.

I was stunned. I had never seen the movie in color before—I hadn't even known the color version existed—and I was shocked. It dawned on me that even though I'd heard about the Ruby Slippers, the Yellow Brick Road, the Horse of a Different Color, and the Emerald City, from my perspective, those brilliant hues had been hidden in plain sight—which, it turns out, is an apt metaphor for the movie itself.

You know the story: Dorothy is unhappy at home in Kansas, bumps her head, and wakes up in Munchkinland. After Dorothy is lauded as a hero for knocking off the Wicked Witch, she and Toto set off on the Yellow Brick Road, where they're eventually joined by the Scarecrow, the Tin Man, and the Cowardly Lion.

Eventually they make their way to the Emerald City, where they're planning to meet the Wonderful Wizard of Oz and ask him for the things they need: brains for the Scarecrow, a heart for the Tin Man, courage for the Cowardly Lion, and a one-way ticket back to Kansas for Dorothy and Toto.

But before he'll grant their wishes, the Wizard sends them off to fight his archenemy, the Wicked Witch of the West, who's protected by a phalanx of spellbound soldiers and terrifying flying monkeys.

I'll spare you the details of the battle, but Dorothy and her crew eventually defeat the Wicked Witch ("I'm melting,

I'm melting"), free the soldiers from their trance, and return to the Emerald City. There they discover that the Wizard is a phony ("Pay no attention to the man behind the curtain"), and even though he has what Dorothy's companions need—a heart-shaped clock on a gold chain for the Tin Man, a diploma for the Scarecrow, and a medal for the Cowardly Lion—he has no way to get her and her little dog home.

That's when Glenda the Good Witch shows up and tells Dorothy that she has had what she needs within her all along: Dorothy need only click her heels together and repeat, "There's no place like home, there's no place like home, there's no place like home." Hearing this, Dorothy says her good-byes, clicks her heels, and is magically transported back to Kansas, where she wakes from her dream.

But wait just a damn minute. Let's back up to that final scene in the Emerald City where Glenda tells Dorothy how she can get home. Isn't Glenda called the Good Witch? Watch that scene again and I'll bet you'll also wonder how good could she be. If I were Dorothy, I'd be furious: "WTF??!! I had it in me all the time? Then why the hell did I have to travel across this God-forsaken country with these three freaks, fight lions and tigers and bears (oh my), get attacked by man-eating trees, nearly OD on hallucinogenic poppy fumes, get chased by a platoon of freaking flying monkeys, kill two witches for Pete's sake, and then come all the way back here—when I had it with me all along? What kind of crap is that?"

Of course the movie *The Wizard of Oz* is a metaphor for life. Its not so subtle message is that we should be pleased with what we already have because that's what we actually really want. And just in case we viewers aren't savvy enough to grasp the subtext, when Dorothy awakens from her fevered dream, she makes it very clear that the people standing around her bed in Kansas remind her of the different characters she met on her journey from Munchkinland to Oz.

The movie's message—similar to the message of this chapter—is that the answer to figuring out what your brand stands for is hidden in plain sight.

To find it, you just have to follow the Yellow Brick Road.

EVERYTHING IS AMAZING . . . BUT NOBODY'S HAPPY

It used to be that when you were standing around the water-cooler at work, someone would ask, "Did you see so and so on TV last night? She was hilarious." And if you hadn't seen it, chances were you never would. After all, there were occasional reruns, but if you missed those rebroadcasts, you had no way to access programming that had already aired.

When that happens today, you only have to go to YouTube and type a few words into the search box to find almost any clip from almost any show from almost any time. And that's a very good thing because it means you can watch Louis C.K.'s rant on Conan O'Brien's show from February 29, 2009.

Louis C.K. was going on about the most innovative technology of the day, but he was really talking about something much more profound. In his rant, the comedian chastises people who complain that their cell phone communications aren't fast enough by reminding them that the signal "has to go to space and back." Next, he mimics travelers who complain about the minor hiccups of modern air travel, then reminds them, "You're sitting in a chair *in the sky*!"

Louis C.K.'s rant, in addition to accurately portraying many people today, points out how the ubiquity of amazing technology has unfortunately turned so many people into self-centered "Instant-Ons."

Context has power outside the arts and entertainment, however; it also provides a powerful tool for business success. The development of the automobile into the modern device we all depend on illustrates this wonderfully.

THE CONTEXT OF HORSES AND CARS

Because great minds think alike, different people often come up with new inventions at the same time. For example, many different inventors were working on the lightbulb when Thomas Edison cracked the code and produced the first workable electric light. A number of engineers were also working on the wireless radio when Marconi finally figured out how to build one. And a number of inventors, including Adolph Diesel and Gottlieb Daimler, created the modern automobile simultaneously. But Karl Benz received the first patent in 1886 and was producing almost six hundred cars per year before the turn of the century. These innovators created the content of the modern automobile.

But Henry Ford figured out the context.

Before Ford created the automobile's context, the invention had more in common with a jet ski than what we would recognize today as a modern car. The vehicles were custom made and very expensive and used mostly as fun sporting devices rather than as a means of transportation.

The problem was that there simply weren't enough cars on the road for filling stations to proliferate across the country, for roads to be sized and paved for autos, or for mechanics or tire shops to be available wherever drivers needed them. There was no way for automobiles to serve as day-to-day transportation because they weren't ubiquitous. Instead, cars were used for fun outings and not driven further than the capacity of their fuel tank would allow. Of course, if a car broke down away from home, there was usually no way to repair it because trained auto mechanics weren't available. And even if they were, replacement parts couldn't be kept in inventory because they were not interchangeable between the mostly handmade custom cars that required them.

Henry Ford recognized the Catch-22 created by the new car. He saw that automobiles would not become popular until the support services required to make them usable were available everywhere. At the same time, services wouldn't and couldn't become ubiquitous until there were enough cars on the road to justify providing them.

Ford's great breakthrough was to make cars inexpensive enough that most middle-class families could afford them. That way, the required support services would pop up to meet their needs. Understanding this led Ford to develop a number of innovative production techniques that resulted in both lower prices and higher sales.

Everyone's heard the apocryphal line that Ford Model Ts were available in "any color as long as it's black." Why were the cars available with no choice in color? Because having only one paint line in the assembly plant saved money and because

the Japan black lacquer used was the fastest drying paint available, allowing Ford to slash production times.

Ford invented lots of other money-saving techniques and
practices, and he appropriated even more, such as the first
modern assembly line (first employed for automobiles by Ran-
som Olds for his Oldsmobile factory in 1902) and the military
advance of using interchangeable parts. Ford also figured out
strategies for using his vendors to lower his prices. Besides being
a merciless negotiator, Ford insisted on requirements and speci-
fications from his vendors that helped his company save money
and produce more cars for less. For example, he demanded his
vendors construct the pallets on which they delivered their parts
out of certain woods cut to very specific dimensions. His work-
ers would then disassemble the pallets, sand the wood smooth,
and reuse it for the floorboards in the Model Ts.

But Ford's most important innovation was employing his
vision to craft his future. He understood that in order to change
the automobile's context, he couldn't simply build his cars to
meet his potential consumers' needs; instead he had to create
a new reality. As Ford famously said, "If I asked my customers
what they wanted, they would have said 'faster horses.'"

Coincidentally, the leading entrepreneur of the twenty-
first century, Apple founder and CEO Steve Jobs, echoed
Ford's words almost a hundred years later when he said, "People don't know what they want until you show it to them."
And "so you can't go out and ask people, you know, what's
the next big [thing]?"

Of course Ford's and Job's visionary accomplishments had
more than this in common. In 1903, the president of Michigan
Savings Bank advised Henry Ford's lawyer against investing in

the Ford Motor Company with the admonition, "The horse is here to stay but the automobile is only a novelty—a fad." And in 1977, only seven years before Apple introduced the Macintosh computer, Ken Olson, chairman and founder of Digital Equipment Corporation, addressed the World Future Society with the words, "There is no reason for any individual to have a computer in his home." Clearly both of these men were looking at the content, not the context, of the inventions they were disparaging.

In 1907, the Winton Motor Carriage Company ran an ad with the headline "Dispense with a Horse and Save the Expense, Care and Anxiety of Keeping It." As quaint and archaic as this sounds, think about how this ad would work today. Simply replace the word "horse" with the word "car" and it could very easily be an ad for the ride-sharing app Uber: "Dispense with a Car and Save the Expense, Care and Anxiety of Keeping It."

While it looks like Uber is competing with the taxi industry, the company is in fact disintermediating the practice of private car ownership. Sure, Uber drivers have to own their own cars today, but that's just a temporary situation. As autonomous vehicles become the norm, Uber's service will operate without any human drivers at all. And if you take an even deeper look at the technologies Uber is both disseminating and perfecting, you'll see that the company is not just adept at moving people: Uber is creating the logistics systems necessary to deliver all sorts of products now being handled by other technologies and other companies.

The key to the Winton Motor Carriage Company's and Uber's messages is not the function of their respective transportation devices: a horseless carriage for Winton or a privately owned shared car for Uber. Instead it's the context that the devices operate in. Most horses and cars are perfectly capable of getting their operators from point A to point B, as are the replacements that the advertisers are offering. But it's the nonfunctional emotional stimuli that most affect users' willingness to continue to engage with the device: in both cases the expense, care, and anxiety of ownership.

Speaking of transportation devices, do you remember the first time you rode a bike all by yourself? I remember when I did as if it happened yesterday.

THE DAY EVERYTHING CHANGED

I hopped up on the shiny blue two-wheeler I got for my birthday and pumped my legs furiously while I struggled to keep the wobbling handlebars pointing straight down the street. All the while my dad ran alongside me holding onto the saddle and keeping me and the bicycle upright.

At some point my dad quietly let go of the seat and let me ride off on my own. I shot down the street without a care in the world until I looked back and realized my dad wasn't there keeping me steady anymore—in fact he was standing about a block back, catching his breath and watching me ride away. That was about the time that the wobbly handlebars and gravity won the battle, and I went crashing to the pavement.

It was almost exactly the same story some thirty years later when I taught my son to ride his bike. He fought with the handlebars and wobbled along and spent some time sprawled out on the pavement, just as I had done all those years earlier.

But before too long, Danny figured out how to control his bike, and his life changed forever. All of a sudden he could get to his friends' houses by himself or ride to the park on his own.

He was free.

A few years later I taught my daughter to swim. She'd stand on the side of the pool while I bobbed in the water just a few feet away from the rim. With an excited, "Ready, Daddy?!" and a big flap of her little arms, she'd hurl herself into the air and splash down into the water, where she'd leave a lacey trail of bubbles straight down to the bottom. Ali would stay there until I'd dive down to grab her and bring her up to the surface. After taking a big breath and flashing an even bigger smile, she'd shove her wet curls off her face and squeal, "Again, Daddy!!" and we'd repeat the whole process over and over.

After a few weekends of this, Ali figured out the secret to buoyancy and would splash into the pool and dog-paddle all the way over to me without plummeting to the bottom. Now she could go to swim parties at friends' houses and run along the surf at the beach without worrying about touching the water.

Life was never the same again.

The ancient Greeks called that instant of critical discovery where everything changes *anagnorisis*; Malcolm Gladwell calls it "the tipping point"—the momentary catalytic mechanism that introduces a whole new world of clarity, opportunity, and possibility. Steering a bike without your mom or dad holding onto the seat and swimming on the top of the wa-ter instead of sinking to the bottom both require a leap of faith and some new skills. But in both cases, figuring out the counterintuitive solution makes all the difference and changes everything.

Building your All About Them brand is just like that. Once you create a compelling brand, you reach your own tipping point and everything changes. The big question is, How do you achieve this?

Ahhh, that's where the branding process becomes counterintuitive and—just like riding a bike or swimming in the pool—requires new skills.

Most people who don't know better talk incessantly about their product: how many locations a retailer has; how powerful its computers are; how long the company's been in business; *se habla español*. The problem is that nobody cares about those things until they're interested in the product or service in the first place. As Theodore Roosevelt said, "No one cares how much you know until they know how much you care."

You're not interested in how many bottles of wine are available on the menu of a restaurant you're not planning to visit. You don't care how inexpensive a pair of running shoes is if you don't even want to try them on. It doesn't matter how many lawyers work for a firm you've never heard of and will never hire. You don't care about the gas mileage of a car you're never going to drive or the fit of a suit you're never going to try on.

Please don't misunderstand: all of those product attributes are critical to performance and satisfaction. But they're what we call "reasons to believe" (RTBs) and are of no interest or consequence to your potential customers until those customers are interested in your product.

Instead, the real value of your product or service lies in the understanding and promotion of the context within which you operate. Learning to ride a bike is not about understanding gear ratios or wheel diameter; it's about freedom. Picasso's sculpture is not about one piece of junk being welded to another in a clever manner; it is about the state of Spain's transformation. Even Louis C.K.'s rant was not really about the transmission speed of cellular telephones or airplane flights from New York to Los Angeles; it was about how we value what those technologies help us achieve.

Separating the emotional appeal from the functional benefits of what we offer is one way to add value to our products and services without changing their operational efficiency. And one of the best ways to do this is to become a "SPOC."

ARE YOU A SPOC?

My mortgage company made a mistake.

For some odd reason it did not have a record of my windstorm insurance certificate on file and went out and bought a windstorm policy for my home. I live in Miami, and windstorm insurance is very important because we've had some devastating hurricanes. Thanks to our storm history, mortgage companies have stringent requirements about the amount and type of insurance that must protect the homes they finance. And as you might expect, windstorm insurance in South Florida can be very expensive. Worse, it becomes especially costly when it's a forced purchase and the bank buys it for you with no care for the cost. So when I opened the form letter from my mortgage company explaining that it had purchased a windstorm insurance policy for me, I was both surprised by the error and stunned by the cost.

But I didn't call my mortgage company to get this problem corrected because I knew that would require interminable waits on the phone, frustrating conversations with lots of uninterested people, and the faxing—and refaxing—of a giant stack of forms and documents to prove that I had already purchased the required windstorm insurance.

Instead, I simply scanned the form letter the bank sent me and e-mailed it to my insurance agent with a note scribbled on the bottom of the page: "Please take care of this for me. Thank you."

His response was short and sweet: "No worries, I'll handle. No need for you to be involved. Have a great day."

My insurance agent is my SPOC.

My wife, Gloria, is a very committed and talented nurse practitioner. When she's not providing hospice care to her end-of-life patients, she works in a concierge medical practice where the practitioners take extremely good care of their charges. Her medical office does this by providing everything patients need to stay as healthy as possible—from checkups to exams to treatments and almost everything else. And when those patients need special diagnoses or treatments that her office does not provide, Gloria's medical office still handles its patients' needs by referring them to the best specialists. Of course, the practice also follows up with the specialists' offices to make sure those patients' problems have been properly managed.

Unlike many medical offices, where hour-long waits in the waiting room and rushed fifteen-minute visits with a harried doctor are the norm, my wife's office is a peaceful oasis where patients with appointments are seen almost immediately. Gloria and the physicians she works with spend as much time as necessary with each and every patient and do whatever it takes to best solve their health problems.

My wife's officemates might not know it, but they are SPOCs too.

When a car breaks down on the side of the road, most people pop the hood and stare at the engine, vainly looking to see what's wrong. Then they either call Triple A or a tow truck and deal with the annoyance of getting their car to a mechanic and the cost of getting it repaired.

But when my friend Mike's car broke down, he didn't do any of those things. Instead, Mike called the salesman at the dealership he bought the car from and explained his predicament. Mike's salesman not only sent a truck and a mechanic to pick up Mike's car but also arranged to bring him a loaner so he could continue on with his day.

My friend Mike buys and leases all of his Mercedes-Benzes from our local dealer. And when I say "all of his Mercedes-Benzes," I mean a lot of very special cars because my friend Mike is an extremely successful serial entrepreneur and buys lots and lots of cars from the dealership. Mike tells me that he does business with this particular Mercedes-Benz dealer because it takes care of everything he needs. He knows its prices are good, but he also knows that whatever he requires will be taken care of quickly and easily. Granted, Mike is an especially loyal and valuable customer to the dealership, but it in turn provides him with a level of customer service that separates its business from most of the average dealerships out there.

And Mike's salesperson understands that the specific brand attribute that keeps Mike coming back to buy his cars from that dealership is not simply the performance or the status of a Mercedes-Benz but the carefree ownership experience the company provides.

Mike's Mercedes-Benz salesperson and his dealership are SPOCs.

In this day and age, when all pricing and product information is just a click of the mouse away, you really have very few distinctive options to grow your business. You can lower your prices so that people will do business with you because you're so cheap (not a particularly healthy way to run a company, by the way), you can offer something that no one else does (a specialty, a patented process, an unbeatable location, special software, or the competitive advantage of size or critical mass), or you can develop a brand that adds extreme value to your offerings.

But while you're doing these things, you can also do what my insurance agent, my wife's medical practice, and Mike's Mercedes-Benz dealer have all done. You can be a SPOC and eliminate the need for your customers to ever call your competition.

SPOC is a simple acronym that stands for "single point of contact." By doing everything so competently and so comprehensively for their clients and customers, SPOCs create a powerful vacuum that leaves no room for competition to sidle in. By becoming single points of contact, SPOCs demonstrate their value in an All About Them manner.

I have no need to talk to the other insurance agents who constantly court me because I know that not only are my family and my assets well covered, but I don't have to lift a finger to make sure everything runs smoothly. My insurance SPOC is so committed to building this bond of trust that he even fixes problems he didn't cause, such as the mistake my mortgage company made. And he knows me well enough to know I'm not interested in what goes on behind the scenes, so he doesn't need to impress me with how much work was required on his part. He only needs to say, "No worries, I'll handle. No need for you to be involved. Have a great day," for me to be satisfied.

Attaining SPOC status is not easy, and it's not for the lazy or faint of heart. But it is a very profitable and sustainable way to run your business. And in this day and age of constant change and upheaval, that's a very powerful position to be in.

Being a SPOC is a powerful All About Them strategy because it tells your customers that your business exists to make their lives better. Like the Picasso sculpture and Ford's auto factories, this strategy focuses on the context of the situation your customers operate in and directs all of the focus onto them in a positive, memorable, and satisfying way.

Just like learning to swim or to ride a bike, learning to make your brand All About Them changes everything. And once you figure that out, nothing will ever be the same again.

THE GBM MOMENT

When Edgar Allan Poe characterizes his distraught murderer in "The Telltale Heart" as knowing what the old man with the "vulture-eye" (his victim) felt, the suspense writer describes physical sensations to depict a condition and set a mood. Autological terms such as "spine-tingling" and "backbreaking" give us deeper understanding of a situation because we not only read the words and comprehend their meaning but also feel what the author is trying to convey.

You've heard people talk about knowing something "in their gut." Or someone's told you how a potentially dangerous setting made "the little hairs on the back of his or her neck stand up." Maybe you've described a special moment by telling a friend how your "eyes welled up" or how your heart was "bursting with pride."

The addition of physical sensations makes our experiences—both lived and listened to—more robust and relatable. The feelings also enrich our understanding and fortify it with a non-intellectual emotional richness that we wouldn't enjoy from an intellectual explanation alone.

Marketing, too, uses sensations to get us to respond to its messaging. The classic Alka-Seltzer commercial line "I can't believe I ate the whole thing" brilliantly contrasted the queasiness of indigestion with the soothing fizzy sounds of the two antacids dissolving in a glass of water. More recently, the ALS Ice Bucket challenge married the fun of daring your friends to do something slightly uncomfortable with the democratized distribution power of social media. But the videos of people dumping ice water on their heads and the grimaces they made helped the ALS Association raise an unprecedented $220 million around the world. How successful was the campaign? During the same period the year before introducing the challenge, the association received just $2.5 million in charitable donations.

This revelatory sensation—the prompt when noticeable physical sensations lead to deeper enjoyment and engagement—is called the goose bump moment (GBM). It is the exact instant when the race is won, the deal is struck, the argument is accepted. And even if selection and payment come later, the GBM tells the customer that he is going to buy this product. It's almost as if the raising of goose flesh on your arms (or the little hairs on the back of your neck) is the catalytic mechanism that defines the event instead of the result of whatever it is you've just enjoyed.

Experiencing these aha flashes not only enhances enjoyment of the moment but also creates the memory that will be retold later. Experiences as universal as saying, "I do," or hearing your baby's first word, or as specific as the frighteningly unexpected drop in Disney's Tower of Terror ride etch themselves deep into our memories. And when they do so, they also indelibly attach themselves to the brand value of our understanding—whether it's the way we relate to our marriage, to our children, or to visiting Walt Disney World.

But GBMs don't occur only in dramatic moments. They can be felt and enjoyed anytime a physical sensation helps to define an experience. The pursuit of GBMs explains why Apple spends so much time engineering the satisfying click on its keyboard buttons. It's why Lexus weights the doors of its luxury cars to close with an effortless yet fulfilling "thunk." It's why Edy's churns its ice cream to be creamier and Perrier-Jouët ages its champagne to be bubblier.

It's why the Nordstrom sales associate walks around the cash-wrap desk to hand you your purchase and why e-cigarettes glow blue when smokers draw on them. The desire to create GBMs is why Harley-Davidson motorcycles are so loud and why Teslas are so quiet. Quite simply, GBMs are why we can't stop popping the bubble wrap.

Although these experiences are different, you may have noticed that all of them use the same overall technique: they all engage our senses. And while some products' GBMs engage the specific sense they are purchased to enhance—the tasty sting of Tabasco, say, or the thumping bass of an Earth, Wind, & Fire song—often the sensual cue is not directly related to the product's function. A good example is a car door's slam, indicating quality and solidity to a potential buyer shopping in the dealership.

Creating a GBM can be as time-consuming and expensive as Rolls-Royce's painstakingly installing 1,340 fiber-optic bulbs in the $12,000 starlight leather headliners of its Wraith two-door coupe (believe it or not, this can cost even more if buyers request that the ceiling re-create the constellation of a specific place in the world or time in history). Or a GBM can be as easy to engineer as sprinkling fresh herbs or sea salt on your morning omelet.

Speaking of food and the GBMs created by taste and smell, here's a simple way to transform an everyday experience into something greater. Because smell is known to enhance the appetite and please the senses, simply mixing a dash of cinnamon with the ground beans in their coffeemakers, professional offices and retail stores alike can create a powerful GBM for their customers and employees.

Although considered common today, cinnamon is actually a powerful superfood with a fascinating and compelling history. Not only has it been shown to help control blood sugar in type 2 diabetics, but tests have also shown it to have favorable effects on cholesterol and triglycerides. Other studies have shown cinnamon to reduce the pain of headaches and help test subjects focus and concentrate. Olfactory scientists even believe that cinnamon's scent can produce feelings of elation.

But in Europe's Middle Ages cinnamon was a rare and highly sought status symbol because of its unique ability to preserve meat and mask the smell of decay. It was so valuable that the Portuguese conquered Ceylon (present-day Sri Lanka) specifically to control the manufacture and importation of the spice. Christopher Columbus even promised Queen Isabella that he had discovered cinnamon in the new world, a guarantee that turned out to be false. Regardless of its history, however, using the spice to warm up an environment is an easy and inexpensive way to create a simple GBM in your store or office.

Speaking of easy and inexpensive ways to create simple GBMs, read this text message that my friend Soren Thielemann, a very talented art director, sent me:

> Good morning Bruce. I'm at a small café in Lauderdale-by-the-Sea and their door handle put a smile on my face. All they did was remove the standard knob from the door and replace it with a baker's whisk. What fun! I haven't tasted the food or had a sip of their coffee yet but I already like this place. It's the power of a first impression and the impact of a creative surprise.

I appreciate not just the attention to detail on the door handle but the obvious delight that went into creating and sharing it. I also like that the establishment not only crafted a delightful little introduction to its café but demonstrated how simple and inexpensive it can be to work a powerful GBM into your business.

Delight is such a simple thing to share and enjoy but seems so hard to make time for, especially in a commercial environment. And yet, when it crosses our path, we know something special has happened, and we remember it fondly.

I remember waiting in line for a sandwich at a local restaurant when an apron-clad cook came out of the kitchen and handed us small paper cups filled with steaming samples of the soup of the day.

I remember when the Wilford-Brimley-lookalike stable hand at a Yosemite equestrian center showed me how to find my way down to the lake to read my book while my wife and kids went horseback riding (I've been on horseback twice in my life—the first time and the last time!).

I remember the last solo in Vince Gill's song "Jenny Dreamed of Trains," where the guitar player sneaks the melody of Elizabeth Cotton's "Freight Train" into the closing refrain.

It's that gracious gesture, what Cajuns call "lagniappe," that turns an ordinary occurrence into a memorable one and creates a GBM. It's the surprise you find in the bottom of the Cracker Jack box, the spontaneous smile on Julia Roberts's face when Richard Gere snaps the jewelry box shut in *Pretty Woman*, the complimentary copy of *Winnie the Pooh* that came with your iPad, the rainbow after a rainstorm, the dollar bill found in an old pair of pants, or the Beatles' song "Her Majesty," which played fourteen seconds after "The End" on *Abbey Road* (when you were already disappointed that the album was over).

Small delights are often free, usually lighthearted, and almost always unexpected. In fact, they seem to show up and matter most when things look a bit bleak and gray (on a crowded airplane, following a dreary and wet thunderstorm, after the last song of a great Beatles album, and so forth).

Small delights are hard to create but easy to identify. Most importantly, they are an incredibly cheap way to build customer satisfaction and encourage repeat usage.

Utilizing physical sensations to enhance the desirability of a product or service is clearly a viable All About Them technique. And by finding ways to incorporate those cues, you can build your brand value with small delights and GBMs.

THE POWER OF WORDS

Randy Gage taught me how to deliver a keynote speech.

Gage's main point? A keynote speech is about a single thought you want your audience to follow, understand, and learn.

His supporting evidence? The name "keynote speech."

According to Gage, the word "keynote" explains exactly what the presentation should be: a speech conveying a single message—a key note speech. Get it? Once you see Gage's way, could it be any clearer?

Because I've been lucky enough to appear on Melissa Francis's show and others on the FOX Business channel a few times a week, friends call me when they get the opportunity to be on TV. I don't do media training, but I've attended enough of it—and been on TV enough now—that I can sometimes make some useful recommendations.

One thing that's become clear to me is that the interviewer on whatever show I'm lucky enough to appear on actually represents the viewers themselves. Johnny Carson represented a wide swath of the American audience back when advertisers cared about white middle-class viewers. Larry King appealed to so many viewers because he was an "everyman" (just a big clumsy schnook like the rest of us) in awe of the celebrities he was interviewing. Oprah Winfrey represented an emerging new audience, not just African American but female and empowered.

Anderson Cooper looks young enough to be handsomely aspirational to middle-aged viewers but with a headful of gray hair so we can relate to him. Bill O'Reilly—the interviewer whose brand essence is most congruent with his viewers' wants and needs—regularly roughs up his mostly urban, mostly educated, and mostly affluent guests simply because his audience would like to beat them up too but cannot. And on the other end of the spectrum, my friend Melissa Francis is so warm and gracious that she always makes her guests look smart and witty (as long as they've done their homework and are telling the truth).

This didn't strike me until I was in front of the camera more than one hundred times. But according to Randy Gage's insight, the title "interviewer" should have clued me in immediately. The interviewer is the filter between the guest and the audience. The word's key components—"inter" and "view"—tell you so.

Onomatopoeia is the formation of a word from a sound that resembles what the word means: sizzle, swoosh, and hiss are good examples. Advertisers have taken advantage of these mnemonic devices for years, probably most famously in the classic Alka-Seltzer jingle "Plop, plop, fizz, fizz, oh what a relief it is." You don't just hear the words; you actually hear the pills splashing and effervescing to make you feel better.

But in the case of the compound words "keynote" and "interviewer," we have something more: these words don't sound like what they mean; they are actually made of the words that represent their meaning.

A little searching to better understand onomatopoeia led me to the definition of literal language. Wikipedia describes it as "words that do not deviate from their defined meaning," which would explain the roots of both terms.

The accurate and specific use of literal language is not always so obvious. For example, we regularly use the words "aesthetic" and "anesthetic" without noticing the relationship between the two. "Aesthetic" relates to pleasing the senses, whereas "anesthetic" has to do with shutting off or deadening the senses. Simply adding the "a" or "an" to the root "esthetic"—defined as "concerned with beauty or the appreciation of beauty"— makes the words' meaning that much more precise.

Of course, taking language literally would not always be a positive thing. How many investment or real estate brokers would want to suggest that they make their clients broker? How many consultants would want to be known as sultan(t)s of cons? Perhaps it's good that while we don't see the meanings hidden in some words, we also don't see the negative implications lurking in others.

What's more fascinating to me is that these meanings and implications, hidden in plain sight, add richness to our conversations and help to build our brands. And so do the stories we use these words in.

There's another way to create GBMs, and it can be just as powerful as the effect of spicy flavors or hip-shaking music: it's selling stories.

THE POWER OF THE MASTERMIND

I'm sitting in the executive conference room of the Wayne Huizenga School of Entrepreneurship at Nova Southeastern University in Davie, Florida. Sitting around the giant conference room with me are most of the entrepreneur members of The Strategic Forum (TSF).

I drive up here to Fort Lauderdale at seven in the morning every third Friday to attend the forum's monthly meeting. The organization is a professional group of about forty-five business owners and CEOs who get together to share ideas, help each other network, and listen to an ever-changing roster of business leaders invited to present to the group.

The structure of our meetings is simple. First we go around the room, and all members take a minute or two to introduce themselves and give a very brief overview of their businesses. Then our guests take between twelve and twenty minutes each to present themselves and their businesses.

We ask our guests to talk about three specific things: (1) their journey—that is, how they got to where they are today; (2) their business and what they see happening in their industry and the world; and (3) how our group can help with whatever they are trying to achieve.

Throughout the year we sponsor informal "mini-meetings" where seven to ten members get together for lunch and conversation. Often a member will use these little get-togethers to ask for specific advice or maybe vet a new business plan. The beauty of the group is both the brainpower in the room and the brutal honesty that only friendship and the desire to see everyone succeed can generate.

Twice a year we sponsor a networking cocktail party. And once a year we plan an offsite retreat at which our group spends a weekend listening to great speakers and getting to know each other better.

We also share our meeting with the best students of Nova's Huizenga School of Business MBA program. These outstanding students sit around the room, audit the meeting, and even present themselves and their resumes to the group. We work with the students by providing mentors, a scholarship program, and a postmeeting debriefing class where we discuss how the students can benefit from the group itself and the lessons learned. Most impressively, we even have one MBA student who presented his company to our association a few years ago as a guest, then participated in the student group because, after building a very successful business, he decided to go back to school and get his master's degree; now he sits around the big table as a full member.

The Strategic Forum was not my idea. Jeff Meshel, author of *The Opportunity Magnet*, started the original group in New York City. Meshel's mantra is to positively exploit "the power of the platform" and build an organization whose members focus intensely on helping each other. After attending a New York meeting, my longtime friend and client Seth Werner had the brainstorm of expanding the group to South Florida. But TSF certainly wasn't the first business organization to bring members together with the express purpose of helping each other. Groups like ours have been around for a long time. As far as I can determine, the concept reaches all the way back to Napoleon Hill's concept of the "master mind principle," introduced in his 1937 best-seller *Think and Grow Rich*. Hill didn't claim to have come up with the idea either; rather, he said he was writing about a best practice he had witnessed or participated in.

But even though I didn't think of it first, The Strategic Forum has been a very important part of my professional success and personal happiness. When I was invited to cofound the Florida Forum over twelve years ago, I did it for purely mercenary reasons: I thought it would help me meet potential clients and find new business.

And it has. My return on investment from TSF has been very good. Our advertising agency has gotten hundreds of thousands of dollars of business from member companies and through the introductions members have provided. But what I didn't expect when we started the forum was the benefit of the intellectual stimulation and camaraderie it has given me. The compelling presentations I've heard from our members and guests can keep me fired up for weeks. Even better, I've made some of my closest friends among the great people I've met. And TSF doesn't just benefit me; besides the business and friendships that many of our members have enjoyed, we can even count one very happy marriage that grew out of our organization's networking opportunities.

The most meaningful part of our meetings is the final activity of each encounter. When our guests are done we go around the room again and trade in the real currency of our little group: a heartfelt thank-you. Each member thanks the other participants for the help they've provided over the last month. Joe thanks Kim for making a business connection. Bill thanks Pablo for helping review an intellectual property contract. Becky thanks Yvonne for recommending an oncologist and using her contacts to help her daughter get a quicker appointment (BTW, we are a confidential organization; none of these names and situations are real). This is where TSF truly demonstrates Meshel's "power of the platform."

The guests who get up and present themselves to us are a who's who of today's business leaders. We've heard from the founder and CEO of a major US airline, billionaire developers, leading medical experts, and even a US Supreme Court justice. We're lucky enough to get to listen to engineers, retailers, consultants, manufacturers, and representatives of most every business and business sector you can imagine. And as you might imagine, all of their stories are fascinating. But their presentation skills are not always as good as their status and accomplishments would lead you to expect.

I always find it amazing that capable business people who have built companies, overcome great odds, and really made a difference in the world can sometimes be so inarticulate.

Don't get me wrong. All of the people who stand in front of our group can speak well and have a good grasp of the information they want to share. The trouble is that many of them have yet to figure out that the best stories are not about the protagonist of the tale itself (in our case, usually the entrepreneur standing at the head of the table). Rather they're about how the tale resonates with the lives and aspirations of listeners. In other words, while we want to hear the narrator's success story, we're really hoping for a story we can relate to and information that we can use in our own lives. We're looking for the "Hero's Journey."

THE POWER OF STORY SELLING

American mythologist and writer Joseph Campbell was best known for his theories on the power of stories and myths throughout history. Campbell's theory of the "monomyth" held that all great myths and stories throughout history are simply variations of one metamyth. Campbell was even able to extend his theory to our belief or disbelief in the existence of God. He said, "God is a metaphor for a mystery that absolutely transcends all human categories of thought, even the categories of being and non-being. Those are categories of thought. I mean it's as simple as that. . . . So half the people in the world are religious people who think that their metaphors are facts. Those are what we call theists. The other half are people who know that the metaphors are not facts. And so, they're lies. Those are the atheists."

Campbell's writings explore myths throughout history and diverse cultures to draw the conclusion that most stories follow a common repeated pattern. In his 1949 book *The Hero with a Thousand Faces*, Campbell named this pattern the "Hero's Journey." This journey establishes both the power of myths and the universally recognizable and understandable identity of people (and, I'd add, companies and brands).

Campbell's "Hero's Journey" follows twelve replicable steps that comprise the template that both creates the hero from Campbell's archetype and also facilitates understanding for the viewer.

Act I: The Departure

1. The Ordinary World. We are introduced to the hero (now simply the protagonist) in his natural environment. This provides an overall understanding of the hero and also the history, culture, and so forth within which this individual developed. At the same time, we are also introduced to the hero's sense of dissatisfaction or ennui that presages his evolution.
2. The Call to Adventure. We witness the events or forces that require the hero to assume his rightful or unanticipated place in history.
3. Refusal of the Call. Either our hero or an influential participant in his life expresses doubt at the hero's suitability to take on the task required by the call.
4. Meeting with the Mentor. Our hero meets the wiser character or force (external or internal) that provides knowledge and insight the hero needs (whether he accepts it at the time or not).

Act II: The Initiation

1. Crossing the Threshold. The hero leaves a comfortable home environment and begins a journey into the unknown.
2. Tests, Allies, and Enemies. Our hero is repeatedly tested and begins to learn whom to trust and whom to avoid.
3. The Approach. The hero and his new allies prepare for action or battle.

4. The Ordeal. The hero comes face to face with and overcomes his greatest fear or weakness. This adversarial experience is usually presaged in step one. After surviving the ordeal and triumphing, the hero emerges with new understanding.

5. The Reward. The hero benefits from overcoming the ordeal but may also risk losing any gains won through conflict.

Act III: The Return

1. The Road Back. The hero returns to his original environment to instill the benefit of what was won or learned through the ordeal. This often culminates in a chase scene or a race against time.

2. The Resurrection. The hero is again challenged, often in a much more severe test than the original ordeal itself. By succeeding at this challenge, the hero is able to resolve the forces that were in conflict at the beginning of the journey.

3. The Return with the Elixir. Our hero, now thoroughly transformed by experience, either returns home or continues on the journey. At the same time, the hero transforms his world in the same manner that he was transformed.

According to Campbell's theory, stories throughout mankind's history have used this template to create drama, explain the unknown, and help the listener make sense of the world. Famous tales as profound as the story of Jesus and popular blockbusters including *Star Wars*, *Lord of the Rings*, and *The Matrix* all follow the pattern of Campbell's "Hero's Journey."

But more than religion and entertainment benefit from the structure that Campbell diagramed. Businesses, too, create mythologies about their founders and products to help create understanding of and desire for their products and services.

Compare Campbell's twelve points with what you already know about Steve Job's life story. Regardless of whether the tale told in books and movies is factually accurate or somewhat apocryphal, you'll find that it fits neatly into the structure we've been discussing.

In Act I, Job's ordinary world was the California of his upbringing. His call to adventure took place in the mountains of Nepal and the apple orchards of Oregon. He found mentors in Bill Hewlett of Hewlett-Packard and John Sculley of Pepsi and camaraderie with Steve Wozniak and his other tech partners.

In Act II, Job's tests included poor sales of his Apple I and II computers and the Lisa, and he was eventually fired from the company he had created and banished from Apple. But he persevered using what he learned with the Lisa and his time at Next and Pixar.

In Act III, Jobs returned to Apple and used his newfound knowledge to create a stunning roster of successes, including the Mac, the iPhone, the iPad, iTunes, the Apple Store, and more.

And in the prototypical ending of the most powerful hero stories, just like Jesus, Jim Morrison, John Lennon, and so many others, Steve Jobs died at the very height of his powers. The words of James Dean, "Live fast, die young, and leave a beautiful corpse," would describe all of them perfectly.

But while Campbell's "Hero's Journey" is a perfect lens through which to understand human fables, stories, and movies, its full twelve steps can be a little cumbersome to use as a template for creating your own defining mythology. Instead we look to humorist Bill Stainton and his abbreviated *Hero's Journey for Dummies*.

THE HERO'S JOURNEY FOR DUMMIES

Bill is a twenty-nine-time Emmy Award–winning television producer and humorist who has written for HBO, NPR, and *The Tonight Show with Jay Leno*. I was lucky enough to meet him in Las Vegas at the National Speakers Association Laugh Lab, a semiannual event held to teach professional speakers and presenters how to use humor on the dais.

Bill started his presentation by introducing Campbell's "Hero's Journey" and showing us how it could help speakers create great stories. But because of his experience working in television, Bill understood that the classic format of Campbell's template required too much time for most people to use on a regular basis. And so he showed us his edited version, which required only three steps, brilliantly titled "The Beginning," "The Middle," and "The End."

In "The Beginning" you introduce your hero and put him in a dangerous, uncomfortable, or unpleasant situation, or as Bill called it, "Getting him up a tree." This should take up about 20 to 25 percent of the story. The important thing here is to make sure you capture your listener's interest. So instead of saying, "I was cooking dinner," for example, you might say, "This was the day that I was meeting my fiancé's parents for the first time, and nothing could go wrong," or "I had just invited my biggest client over for dinner, and everything had to be perfect."

Next comes "The Middle." This is where you "throw rocks at your hero" to create what Bill called "the oh crap! moment." Elevating the situation should take about 50 percent of the story.

Finally, you conclude with "The End." Here you let the hero down out of the tree and resolve the story.

In order to use this expedited outline, Bill lays out five steps to help you build your story:

1. Ask the magic question. Don't ask when something great happened or when something funny happened; ask when something went wrong. This is where you find the foundational theme you can build your myth on.

2. Channel your inner Joe Friday and list "just the facts, ma'am." You're not trying to embellish history; you're just establishing what your audience needs to know to gain deeper understanding.

3. "Fertilize" the tale (or "plant the crap," as Bill put it). This is the tipping point after which nothing will ever be the same again. For example: "I dropped to the floor and my heart stopped beating." "That's when I found out my parents weren't married." "The lawyer told me that our patents hadn't been filed."

4. Next you need to escalate the conflict (in Bill's words, "Go rock collecting and throw the rocks at your hero"). Here you continually pile on bad news until it seems the hero simply won't be able to emerge from the situation at all, let alone emerge victorious.

You may not be aware of it, but you've seen this technique used many times before. Rewatch Dustin Hoffman in *Tootsie*, and you'll see how the writers continually added to his character's burdens as the story rolled along. Tom Cruise's character in *Risky Business*, Matthew Broderick's character in *Ferris Bueller's Day Off*, and Bill Murray's character in *Groundhog Day* all endure the same situation. Closer to home, just turn back to Chapter 1 of this book and reread about my road-to-Damascus moment, and you'll see how my situation at the book signing just continued to get worse and worse (the sharp reader will realize that I constructed that tale, along with others in this book, based on Bill's template).

The key to this section is not only continually piling on the troubles but making one assault on the hero flow seamlessly into the next. If you can characterize one rock as the consequence of another that your audience has learned about but may have forgotten, so much the better.

5. Finally you UPS the story and ship it home—wrap it up and tie a bow around it. It's time to show what the hero learned, how it changed him, and how your listener can benefit from the hero's experience.

By doing this, not only do you get the opportunity to tell your prospects why they should be doing business with you, but you also give them a way to explain your product or service to anyone they might have to answer to. And by making the story as entertaining as possible, not only do you capture their interest and make it easier for them to remember your words, but you also allow them to retell the story with the same relish and enthusiasm that you did.

Don't be surprised if you hear your tale being retold with a little extra embellishment, a little more fanfare, a little additional oomph. This is what Bill Stainton calls "the Silly Putty effect."

Remember those Sundays when you used to stretch out on the family room floor with the comic section and a blue plastic egg filled with Silly Putty? You'd open the newspaper to your favorite cartoon and flatten a big wad of putty on it, hammering down with your fist. Next you'd carefully peel the putty off the newspaper, taking a thin layer of the colorful ink with it.

On the flip side of the flattened pancake of Silly Putty, you'd have a mirror image of the comic strip. Then you'd stretch and pull the putty until you'd contorted the characters' faces to ridiculous proportions (my daughter has an app on her phone that does the same thing with photographs, but it's not nearly as satisfying). As you stretched the putty, the images got funnier and funnier until eventually you'd pull too far, and the sheet of putty would snap in half.

Your stories will be just like that. When you do a good job of creating and telling your tale, the people who repeat it will act just like they've captured your story on Silly Putty.

They'll unconsciously experiment with stretching it and altering it, learning just how far they can exaggerate your tale before it snaps.

What matters here is not that they embellish your story but that they make it their own. Because in the retelling not only are they introducing someone else to your idea and your brand, but they are simultaneously evangelizing them. By doing this, your listeners create their own All About Them environment where they add as much of their own personality to your tale as needed to make it fit into their worldview.

This is where storytelling magically transforms into story selling.

HOW A TEN-MINUTE PITCH TURNED INTO A $100 MILLION BUSINESS

Remember Bill Stainton's recommendation not to look at the sublime moments when everything was going your way but to ask, "When did something go wrong?" Through this universally understandable bit of the human experience, your hero, and thus your brand, becomes the relatable champion that your audiences want to interact with.

Consider the almost prototypical rags-to-riches story of Jamie Kern Lima and her company, IT Cosmetics.

Like so many fledgling entrepreneurs, Lima had invested everything in her big idea. She had quit her job as a local news anchor and started her business at the kitchen table of her Studio City, California, apartment. Although Lima believed that QVC was the perfect venue to present her Bye Bye Under

Eye Concealer to the world, she was not able to get the retail network to pay any attention.

Eventually Lima's perseverance paid off. She was displaying her products at a cosmetics trade show in Manhattan when QVC network executives happened by and expressed interest in airing her line. And this is where everything changed for Lima and IT.

In an interview for *Entrepreneur Magazine* about Lima's extraordinary success, Doug Rose, the senior vice president of marketing and programming for QVC, said, "Our customers are shopping not so much because of a desire to buy something as they are engaged in learning about what's new, meeting interesting people and hearing their stories. We talk a lot about storytelling being one of our superpowers as a retailer."

Of course Lima's products were well designed, well packaged, and well priced. After all, she created them with the help of plastic surgeons. And of course Lima's experience as an on-air personality went a long way to helping her best present her products and her story to the QVC audience. But it was Lima's story, her hero's journey, that ultimately accelerated her enormous success.

As *Entrepreneur Magazine* describes it, because she "suffers from severe rosacea and lost her eyebrows in her thirties, Lima . . . devised a demo in which she wipes off her brows on-air and then pencils them back on with IT Cosmetics' Brow Power."

Since her first time on QVC, Lima has logged over seven hundred appearances on the network, and her company's annual sales have ballooned to over $100 million.

Certainly Lima's story is both compelling and heartwarming, and her ability to tell her unique tale creates a performance that's hard to turn away from. But it's the empathy that her tale prompts in the viewer that makes it so easy to relate to and so hard to ignore.

"It's not just a sales thing," Lima says. "By me taking off my makeup and showing my rosacea or showing that I have no brows, I hope that women feel better about their own issues, because everyone has them."

Of course you know that not all of the women who spent more than $100 million buying IT Cosmetics suffer from the same skin problems that Jamie Kern Lima does. Instead they relate to Lima's hero's journey and see themselves and their own problems mirrored in the context (not necessarily the content) of her issues. By building an All About Them brand, Jamie Kern Lima not only built an incredibly profitable empire but made a difference in the outer and inner lives of her customers.

You can too.

4

WHAT WE SELL VERSUS
WHAT WE EXCHANGE FOR MONEY

ATTORNEY'S FEES

A man phoned a lawyer and asked, "How much would you charge for just answering three simple questions?"

"One thousand dollars," the lawyer answered.

"One thousand dollars!" exclaimed the man. "But that's very expensive isn't it?"

"It sure is," replied the lawyer. "Now what's your third question?"

WHAT'S IN THAT CAN OF SOUP YOU JUST BOUGHT?

Believe it or not, soup companies don't sell soup; they sell love. Cans of soup are simply what they exchange for money.

Imagine this commercial: Pretty blonde mid-century mom is puttering around the traditional kitchen. Close your eyes and you can see it: a 1950s space-age-looking Amana range and refrigerator, dark wood cabinets, and yellow Formica counter-tops covered with brightly colored packages of Wonder Bread and Skippy peanut butter. Mom's got her hair in an updo and is wearing a brightly checkered apron over a colorful dress and sensible shoes. She's got a bow in her neatly coiffed hair and a smile on her glossy red lips.

Every once and a while, Mom looks up from her cooking and glances outside. She smiles when she sees little Johnny playing happily in the snow.

Before long she hears a knock on the door and turns to see little Johnny wiping the frost off the windowpane and peering inside. She opens the door and lovingly brushes the snow off little Johnny's knit cap while he rubs his glove under his runny nose. Mom smiles beatifically at Johnny, gives him a lipsticked kiss on the forehead, and guides him to the kitchen table. She pulls off his cap, tousles his hair, and sits little Johnny down to a steaming hot bowl of chicken noodle soup.

Awwwwww. Isn't she a loving mom?

No, she's a lazy mom. All she did was open a can of who-knows-what chemicals, zap it in the microwave, and slap it down on the table.

But of course that message wouldn't sell cans of soup, would it? Instead, Johnny slurps down a hearty spoonful while his mom smiles happily and the touching music reminds us that this is what love is all about. And love is worth a lot more than a fifty-cent can of soup, isn't it?

Soup companies don't sell soup; they sell love. Soup is simply what they exchange for money.

For more than a century, analog photography worked thanks to a simple chemical reaction: silver nitrate exposed to light and certain other chemicals gets darker. And the more silver in the paper available to react with the developing concentrate, the better the quality of the photographic reproduction. That's why the finest photographic art prints sold to collectors and hanging in art museums are called silver prints.

Because of this, it would have made functional sense for Kodak to advertise that its film and photographic papers had the highest concentration of silver nitrate in the industry. But people didn't buy the company's products for their silver content. Instead they bought Kodak's cameras, films, and photographic supplies to save and protect memories of their loved ones.

Which would you pay more for? A bunch of noxious chemicals you don't understand or pictures of your children when they were adorable little kids? This second offer was so powerful that the phrase "Kodak moment"—Kodak's marketing tagline—entered the common lexicon to describe a personal event that demanded to be recorded for posterity.

With the advent of digital photography, of course, the analog process and the companies that grew out of it, like Kodak, went the way of the dodo bird. But their extinction simply emphasizes the point that people care most about what a product (or service) does to make their lives better, not how or why the product actually works. They don't care how their pictures are created, stored, and shared; they only care that they are. They like technologies that make the ultimate end—the recording and sharing of memories—as easy as possible. Because, as we've already seen, product function has become cost-of-entry.

Why is this the case? Common sense would lead us to believe that the way things work would be of primary importance to the purchaser and user. But again, technological advances have changed this paradigm.

Remember the typewriters we talked about earlier? Regardless of how complicated and sophisticated the typewriters were, it was easy to figure out how they worked: your finger pressed a key, the key moved a lever, the lever struck the ink ribbon, and the ribbon left its imprint on the paper positioned on the roller.

When the devices around us were mechanical, it was easy to see how they worked. More importantly, it was easy to understand how they worked, even if we couldn't build or repair them. The process was simple, clear, linear, and comprehensible.

But modern technology has changed that.

Today's consumer has received pretty much every futuristic gizmo and gadget promised by science fiction movies, TV shows, and books. Star Trek's communicator? Today it's called a smartphone. Dick Tracy's two-way wrist radio? Versions are available at every electronics retailer from Apple, Samsung, Motorola, Casio, LG, and more. Rosie's instant meal machine from *The Jetsons*? Our version is called a microwave oven. Biotech laboratories are even cloning replacement bladders, tracheae, and ears in Petri dishes, for Pete's sake. As far as I can tell, the only science fiction devices we're still waiting for are time machines and personal jet packs.

Sure, every other Fourth of July or so, the US Air Force drags out an old jet pack and flies it around a football field somewhere in the heartland, but that pack costs nearly a million bucks and only goes about fifty feet. And I've recently seen a water-based pack that sucks lake water into a pipe and forces it back out the bottom, propelling its wearer a few feet up in the air. But that invention requires a big lake or bay, and you get all wet and can't fly it in an immaculate tuxedo the way James Bond did in *Thunderball.*

Think about what jet packs could do for us. Regardless of where you live, I'm pretty sure you've bitched about traffic within the last week. But if you had a jet pack, you wouldn't give two hoots about traffic at all. Got parking woes? Let's face it, a jet pack would take up a whole lot less room than your gigantic Cadillac Escalade ESV (or your compact Toyota Prius, for that matter), and you could stash it almost anywhere.

Gas mileage? While I don't imagine my jet pack will be a hybrid or solar powered, if we can figure out the technology to make these things work, I'm sure we can figure out how to make them frugal. And zipping around in our jet packs will mean we won't be wasting gas idling in traffic or at red lights.

Don't worry. I'm not entirely quixotic about my request. I know my jet pack won't work when it rains, and I know it'll be ineffective when I'm traveling with my kids. It also won't work when I have a lot of stuff to carry or when I need to tow the boat. But the rest of the time, I think a personal jet pack is exactly what we all need to get around quickly and easily.

So who can create these for us? Yesterday I needed to look up the gestation cycle of the Byzantine fruit fly, and Google found the answer for me in less than .00002 seconds. If Larry and Serge can figure how to do that, I'm sure they have the smarts and resources to get my jet pack made. I also needed to communicate with my agent, who was vacationing in Athens,

Greece, and I did that in real time right from my computer. The guys who figured out how to make that possible could certainly figure out how to make me a jet pack. And today I parked next to a beautiful new Tesla created by the same guy who came up with PayPal and SpaceX. Surely someone like Elon Musk, who could dream up those things while also serving as the model for Robert Downey Jr.'s character in *Iron Man*, could build my jet pack, don't you think?

Of course, I'd want to brand my jet pack, but the truth is, I don't care who makes it a reality. In a perfect world, I'd like Apple to be involved so it'll look cool, and I'd like Porsche to be involved so it'll be fast. Volvo could help make it safe, and Taco Bell could make it affordable. If Starbucks repaired the jet packs, there'd be a service station on almost every corner, and Swatch could make sure everyone could get one. And Marriott could make sure all jet packs worked the same way, no matter where you were in the world. While I don't really care whose logo is on my jet pack as long as it works reliably and I can afford it, I would pay more for jet packs from those companies—especially after the devices become common and everyone's got one. I don't only want a jet pack; I want a special jet pack.

Am I setting my sights too high? In today's world of CAD/CAM (computer-aided design and manufacturing), it seems like anything that can be imagined can be created. Besides the examples I've already mentioned, our lives are chock-full of modern miracles—from the unbelievable capacity of tiny flash drives to contact lenses to Saran Wrap, which Mel Brooks's 2,000-Year-Old Man said is "the greatest thing mankind ever devised."

Have you seen the YouTube videos of those guys who jump off mountains wearing their flying squirrel suits? They zip around the countryside with nothing more than a lot of courage and some fabric stretched tightly between their legs. I'm thinking we could sign a few of those lunatics up as our test pilots to make sure the jet packs work. After all, if those guys are gutsy enough to jump off mountains in skintight Slankets, they certainly won't be afraid to try out our new jet packs.

If you want a jet pack too, maybe we could start a movement. Perhaps if we demonstrate significant market demand, some forward-thinking engineers will get started and build our jet packs already. All you have to do is tweak Arlo Guthrie's lyrics from *Alice's Restaurant* and replace the title words with "jet pack," and you'll see how we can get it done: "Can you imagine fifty people a day? I said fifty people a day walkin' in *asking for a jet pack* and walking out. And friends they may think it's a movement, and that's what it is, the *jet pack* movement, and all you gotta do is join."

Franklin B. Adams wanted "a good five-cent nickel," Huey Lewis wants "a new drug," King Louie, the orangutan in *The Jungle Book*, wants "to be like you." All I want is a personal jet pack. Is that too much to ask?

ALL ADVANCED TECHNOLOGY IS LIKE MAGIC

Of course, my jet pack rant is satirical, but the point should be clear: Why would a device like a jet pack seem any harder to produce than some of the other technological marvels we all take for granted? Would a jet pack be harder to perfect than 3-D virtual reality goggles? Harder than a smartphone app that can identify any song it hears? Harder than 3-D printing? Because I don't understand how any of them work, I can't see how one is anymore difficult to make than any other. After all, as English author Arthur C. Clarke stated in his third law of prediction, "Any sufficiently advanced technology is indistinguishable from magic."

The trouble with magic is that we want to understand what it is and how it works. But once we peek behind the curtain, we're no longer intrigued or enthralled. Card tricks are like that; sleight of hand too. Our need for understanding and control compels us to try to figure out how things work, but in the case of technological advances, our lack of understanding gets in the way.

Don't make the mistake of confusing knowing how something operates with knowing how it works. Of course you understand how to use your laptop or your smartphone, but you probably don't actually understand what's going on under their slick aluminum skins. Maybe you do know something about how computers work and can describe how all data is reduced to a binary system of zeroes and ones. Does that mean you really understand how Internet search engines can return answers to your queries in less than a tenth of a second?

Our comfort level with the things we don't understand increases with time and regular use. So even though we don't really understand how we can chat with someone halfway around the world in instantaneous real time, we've been using telephones and long-distance phone service for long enough now that we simply take them for granted. And even though we might be amazed that our cousin in Australia sounds like he's "right next door," our astonishment soon gives way to interest in the conversation that the technology makes possible.

But we don't so easily understand where the advancements of current technology can lead us—hence, US Patent and Trademark Office Commissioner Charles H. Duell's apocryphal suggestion that the government close the patent office because "everything that can be invented has been invented." This was back in 1899—long before the advent of the modern airplane, the atomic bomb, movie theaters, space travel, computers, the Internet, and even Jiffy Pop popcorn and the Etch A Sketch. Visionary Arthur C. Clarke encapsulated this phenomenon as well in his first law of prediction: "When a distinguished but elderly scientist states that something is possible, he is almost certainly right. When he states that something is impossible, he is very probably wrong."

So what's the point? Quite simply, all of this reinforces the argument that function is no longer the most important component in establishing a mutually beneficial relationship between a product (or service) and its consumer. And this counterintuitive thinking is equally important when it comes to naming products.

NAMING ALL ABOUT THEM PRODUCTS

Do you remember the first time you ate sushi? I'm not talking about after the Japanese cuisine became a common choice in cities and suburbs; I mean when sushi was still an oddity in the United States and you were still a bit squeamish.

"What??!! Eat uncooked fish? Me? Are you crazy?"

If your experience was anything like mine, that first taste was weird and slimy and, of course, very fishy. And even the searing tsunami of wasabi that burned out my sinuses seconds later didn't do much to make my first bite any less odd.

My next few mouthfuls—and my next few trips to the sushi bar—were equally tentative. It took a while until I was willing to gobble down my meal and even a few more evenings out before I developed a taste for sushi and was enthusiastic about eating it.

Chances are you were more likely to eat it because of its cool, exotic-sounding Japanese name: sushi. What's the chance you would have eaten sushi if it went by a clear description of what's actually on the plate?

Raw dead fish.

Ugh.

Speaking of fish, Patagonian toothfish was considered unsellable overcatch until some marketing maven renamed it Chilean sea bass.

Although it's counterintuitive, nondescriptive names often become more powerful brands than their more self-explanatory counterparts. For example, before 1997 Pierre Omidyar's online superpower eBay was known by the much more illustrative yet less successful AuctionWeb.

So what's in a name?

Did you know that Google's original name was BackRub or that Nike was first called Blue Ribbon Sports? Of course you remember that AOL was America Online, but did you know that first it was called Quantum Computer Services?

Some name changes, such as Datsun becoming Nissan, happen for organizational reasons and don't have much effect, other than costing millions of dollars to reestablish the brand. Other name changes, like Federal Express becoming FedEx, make even more sense in an environment of 140-character tweets and even shorter attention spans. And some names get explained after the fact, sometimes apocryphally—for instance, the name Yahoo! has been said to be an acronym for "Yet Another Hierarchical Officious Oracle" or to stem from founders David Filo and Jerry Yang's appreciation for Jonathan Swift's uncivilized Yahoos in *Gulliver's Travels*.

Some name changes reflect changing times—think Ayds Diet Candies or Isis Chocolates. Andersen Consulting spent an estimated $100 million to escape the taint of its sister firm Arthur Anderson's misdeeds when it became Accenture. Kentucky Fried Chicken looked to push the word "fried" out of its name with the new moniker KFC.

ValueJet changed its name to AirTran after slamming a DC-9 so hard and deep into the Everglades there was almost no debris found at the crash site. That unfortunate example makes me wonder when Malaysia Airlines will announce its name change to shake the lingering specter of losing two planes in 2014 (one over the vast waters of Asia and a second in Ukraine).

Cereal companies change their names to satisfy consumer demands for healthier food. Sugar Smacks became Honey Smacks, then just Smacks, and then reverted to Honey Smacks (probably when someone pointed out that "smack" is common slang for heroin). Sugar Crisp became Golden Crisp, Sugar Pops became Corn Pops, and Sugar Frosted Flakes is now simply Frosted Flakes. Of course, the actual sugar content of the cereals was only slightly reduced, but the word "sugar" was cleanly amputated.

In today's metric-happy world of Internet surveys and copy testing, the critical interplay between names and the products they represent is a chicken-and-egg relationship that's as much art as science. But the next time you give a back-of-the-hand dismissal to the hard work of naming products, think how much you would have enjoyed your last serving of *toro* or *maguro* or *ikura* or *hamachi* if sushi were simply called "raw dead fish."

There was once a store in your neighborhood with the name Strictly Tennis. Everyone knew whom Strictly Tennis catered to and what it sold. But then enough kids started playing soccer that the owners decided to carry cleats and jerseys and changed the name to Strictly Tennis and Soccer, which worked just fine until jogging became all the rage. That's when the store changed its name again—this time to Strictly Tennis, Soccer, and Running. Eventually the name morphed again to Strictly Tennis and More.

But now that people are playing Ultimate Frisbee and going to CrossFit and Zumba, what name will the store use? Does Strictly Tennis and More cover its greater reach? Or do the owners need to change the name again to something altogether different?

In the late 1960s, Al Kooper, Bobby Colomby, and a bunch of jazz cats got together and created Blood, Sweat & Tears— one of the era's five seminal rock-and-roll horn bands. The group was so successful that its eponymous second album not only topped the *Billboard* charts and gave the world three major hits, "You've Made Me So Very Happy," "Spinning Wheel," and "And When I Die," but also beat The Beatles' *Abbey Road* for the Album of the Year Grammy.

One has to wonder, though, if Colomby's virtuoso drumming and the late great Lew Soloff's soaring trumpet solos would have been enough if the band had used the more descriptive name Assorted Bodily Fluids instead.

Marilyn Monroe was born Norma Jeane Mortenson. Tony Curtis was originally Bernard Schwartz. Rock Hudson was Roy Harold Scherer Jr. Martin Sheen was Ramón Antonio Gerardo Estévez. Natalie Portman's last name was formerly Hershlag.

How about Ralph Lauren? Did you know that the superstar of American fashion, the designer who combined American prep with English aristocratic style to create a $7 billion fortune, was born Ralph Lifshitz? What's the chance that international heads of industry would attend Davos or the World Economic Forum dressed in a navy blue Lifshitz? What Oscar-winning actress would sashay across the red carpet resplendent in her of-the-moment haute couture Lifshitz?

His original name reminds me of the old joke, "Hey Ralph, if you're Lipshitz, does your ass speak?"

Clearly a name is critical to business success. Unfortunately, however, there's no secret recipe. In a recent *New York Times Magazine* article on corporate names, naming, and namers, titled, "The Weird Science of Naming New Products," author Neal Gabler pointed out that "there are no naming metrics, no real way to know if a new name helps or hinders."

Sometimes a successful name is instructive and tells the potential customer exactly what a product or company does—think Evernote, Discovery Channel, International Business Machines, or the Museum of Modern Art. But, as we've already seen, function can get in the way of future growth and evolving business opportunities when a company identifies with a descriptive name, such as Strictly Tennis, for example, or Burger King or International Business Machines.

Sometimes a successful name honors a company's founders: Hewlett-Packard, for example, or Porsche or Ferrari. But this only works if founders' names stay free of scandal. The founders of WorldCom (Bernard Ebbers) and Enron (Kenneth Lay and Jeffrey Skilling) didn't lend their names to their companies, while Bernard L Madoff Investment Securities LLC did, yet their disastrous results were the same. And while this book was being written, the jury was still out on what Donald Trump's presidential campaign outbursts would do to his eponymous empire.

Sometimes a name can start off well, but then happenstance can change its meaning or implications. This unfortunate occurrence happened to the aforementioned Ayds Diet Candies and Isis Chocolates as well as the band Anthrax.

Sometimes successful names are fanciful—Google, Starbucks, Twitter, Cisco, Citrix, and so on. The problem, of course, is that it takes a lot of time and money for the consuming public to recognize, understand, and accept a name no one's ever heard before.

But before you think a name makes all that much difference, look at the success of a company like Smucker's. The food giant earns hundreds of millions of dollars selling food with a name so distasteful that its tagline is "With a name like Smucker's, it has to be good."

Still, it's a good thing that Smucker's isn't named Assorted Bodily Fluids.

Or Isis.

Or Lifshitz.

THE DIFFERENCE BETWEEN WHAT
WE SELL AND WHAT THEY BUY

If the advancement of technology has rendered product function redundant and ubiquitous and descriptive names can serve to create more roadblocks to success than they avoid, what are today's consumers buying?

This is the essential question that every marketer must answer in order to position a company for victory. And the specific answer is often as counterintuitive as nondescriptive names can be. We're discovering that what people exchange for money can differ greatly from what they actually are purchasing.

Drop by any Starbucks, and you'll see pretty much the same thing: people sitting inside or out (depending on the store's location and the weather), reading the newspaper, checking their phones, typing away on their laptops, meeting with business associates, or getting together with friends. Inside there's usually a line of people waiting to order espressos or half-caf caramel macchiatos. Starbucks is exchanging money for coffee, but its customers are buying something very different.

For years, many Americans' lives revolved around three main locales: home, the workplace, and what's come to be known as the "third place." Third places were often located at a religious institution, such as a church or synagogue, or perhaps an affinity organization, such as the Elk's Club or the Mason's Lodge or the Veterans of Foreign Wars Hall. Sometimes the third place was the building of an alumni association, like the Harvard Club or the Penn Club, or a social club like the Knickerbocker or Century Club. And sometimes the third place was an activity-based location, such as a bowling alley or tennis, golf, or country club.

But thanks to a number of recent phenomena, including the transience of the American public, people's preference to watch cultural and sporting events on the big screen in their living rooms instead of live, the proliferation of residential swimming pools, the increased cost of both purchasing real estate and maintaining churches and clubs, and the recent reality that fewer and fewer Americans consider themselves religious or affiliate themselves with any specific creed or institution, the popularity of these third places has waned.

But just because the traditional reasons people frequented third places have diminished does not mean that today's consumer doesn't still need a place to go. And with the advent of the freelance economy—where more and more people eschew traditional corporate jobs and offices and instead work wherever they can both plug in their laptops and find a good Wi-Fi connection—this need has become even more pronounced.

And this is where Starbucks found its niche. Panos Mourdoukoutas explained this concept in *Forbes*: "For years, Starbucks marketed itself as a 'third place,' an 'affordable luxury' where people could share and enjoy a cup of coffee with friends and colleagues, away from work and home." And as Starbucks itself says on its website:

> From the beginning, Starbucks set out to be a different kind of company. One that not only celebrated coffee and the rich tradition, but that also brought a feeling of connection. . . .

It's not unusual to see people coming to Starbucks to chat, meet up or even work. We're a neighborhood gathering place, a part of the daily routine—and we couldn't be happier about it.

Starbucks has clearly explained its value strategy in the customer service overview known as the *Green Apron Book*. There it spells out the traits that lead to success within the company. Starbucks's "ways of being" are to "be welcoming, be genuine, be knowledgeable, be considerate, and be involved." You've probably already noticed that Starbucks doesn't list anything about selling coffee or increasing customers' check averages as a means to success. Instead it provides a lovely list of ways to build a better community or a third place. And that's because while the brand's currency is coffee (and its attendant paraphernalia, snacks, and other drinks), its customers come back for the community experience.

Think back to the last time you attended a convention at a major conference hotel, in Orlando or Las Vegas perhaps. If you walked through the lobby on your way to your workshops, you probably noticed people standing in line at the hotel Starbucks waiting to order their favorite blend. Later, when you got up to the meeting room, you probably saw lots of people milling around holding their cherished cups of Starbucks coffee. This all makes sense until you notice that the urns of free coffee that the hotel provides for the meeting attendees have little engraved signs reading, "We proudly serve Starbucks coffee."

If there's free Starbucks coffee in the meeting rooms, why do people stand in line to pay for their own cups? Sure, some people have special preferences and want a flat white or a decaf latte, but lots of people are buying the same coffee they can get for free. Obviously the habit, the sense of place, and the experience of getting their morning jolt from a Starbucks barista are all part of the appeal.

Physicians sell examinations and diagnoses, but their patients purchase peace of mind.

Banks and financial institutions sell safety and security and access to capital, but their depositors and borrowers purchase peace of mind and the promise of a brighter future.

Luxury watch manufacturers sell advanced timepieces, but their customers buy status.

While proper function is a cost-of-entry requirement of the goods and services our customers buy, it is no longer the impetus for them to pull the purchase trigger.

WHEN IS A HAIR SALON NOT A HAIR SALON? WHEN IS A RESTAURANT NOT A RESTAURANT?

When you walk into Junior's in Jupiter, Florida, for the first time, you might be surprised by what you find. The walls are covered with graffiti; the furniture is constructed from red and black leather and industrial diamond-plate steel. And the proprietor wears a short sleeve Harley-Davidson mechanic shirt, undoubtedly selected to show off the tattoos inked up and down both of his arms.

The other heavily tattooed guys milling about wear similar uniforms: jeans or baggy shorts, black T-shirts, baseball caps, and heavy chains. And most of them—Ruben, Jairo, Trix, Chi, and Johnny—will be clutching just-sharpened straight razors or have them at hand in their workspaces.

But the people waiting to be served are not typical hot rod shop customers. Instead they're young boys, businessmen, and suburban mothers and fathers.

That's because Junior's is not a garage or a gang hangout.

It's a hair salon.

No, really.

Further down the Florida coast on the tip of Miami Beach, Joe's Stone Crab Restaurant sells the same thing as Junior's. Not haircuts with an OG garage vibe but the feeling that you're in a special place, part of a club, in the know.

On a Saturday night during tourist season, patrons line up in front of Joe's maître d' stand to put their names on the waiting list. Then they stand patiently, even though they know they might wait for a table for more than three hours. And since Joe's doesn't take reservations, the diners are arguably not there despite the long wait but because of it. After all, there is no shortage of trendy restaurants in the area. But where else can you see and be seen in the ground zero of South Beach?

Joe's and Junior's are thriving businesses created for today's All About Them economy, where what you do is less important than how you do it or who you are.

If you only want your hair trimmed, you can get anything from an $8 clip at a discount cuttery to a $150 coif at an exclusive salon. But if you want something different, if you want something cool, if you want an experience, then you want to go to Junior's.

But don't take my word for it; read how Junior's describes its brand on its website: "Junior's Barber Shop, where Rock-N-Roll sets the tone for this garage inspired tattoo vibin' atmosphere. Junior's is a FULL SERVICE Barber Shop offering everything from children's to men's cuts, to hot towel shaves and we even do custom designs for the edgier folk."

Just as Starbucks's *Green Apron Book* doesn't mention coffee or Frappuccinos, you'll notice that Junior's doesn't say anything about how well its barbers cut hair or how inexpensively. That's because those things don't matter. Junior's is not selling haircuts; it's selling an experience.

Joe's grilled fish is the best in Miami and its fried chicken is the best in the world. But Joe's website doesn't brag about its food any more than Junior's brags about its haircuts. Because just like the hairstyles at Junior's, food at Joe's is currency: it's what the restaurant trades for money, but it's not what its customers are buying. Want proof? Go to the website and you'll find recipes for its most acclaimed dishes, including its Caesar salad dressing, ginger salmon, and famous key lime pie, published right there for all the world—and all its competitors—to copy. If all you want is the food, you can make it yourself. That's not what Joe's is selling.

What you can't make yourself is Joe's atmosphere, its feeling, its vibe. Or as the website says, "It has always been the love of food, family, and friends that has brought in customers and kept them coming."

That, and the spillover crowds that tell you you're somewhere special.

WHAT CAN YOU LEARN FROM COFFEE, HAIRCUTS, AND STONE CRABS?

What does all of this have to do with you and your business? The takeaway is that your business needs to make people feel as special as they do at Starbucks, Junior's, and Joe's. More importantly, it's another clear reminder that people are not buying what you sell; they're buying who you are and how you make them feel. And when you do what Junior's and Joe's have done and provide an All About Them experience, you'll find scores of customers who are hungry for your product.

But ignore this counterintuitive positioning, and you can find yourself stuck in the very same frustrating spot as many other marketers. After a lot of real-world trial and error, they come to understand that consumers are not buying the function of what they're selling. At the same time, while they know the importance of figuring out what their customers want, they also know (as we learned in the previous chapter from both Henry Ford and Steve Jobs) that they can't simply ask customers what they're looking to buy.

So where does that answer come from?

Once again, it comes from an unlikely place: deep within themselves. Or in your case, within you.

5

"HEY, LOOK AT ME" (WE HATE HIM BUT WE BECOME HIM)

PINOCHLE

A group of friends are sitting around the card table.

The first man groans. "Oy."

The second man groans. "Oy."

The third man looks at his friends. "Oy vey," he moans even louder.

Finally the fourth man says, "Hey are we going to play cards, or are you guys just going to keep showing off?"

THE "HEY, LOOK AT ME" KID

Remember the "Hey, Look at Me" kid? We all grew up with him, and we all hated him. He was the one in your class who not only needed to do whatever anyone else was doing but had to do it better and louder, always making sure that everyone else saw what he was up to.

The "Hey, Look at Me" kid was up on the high dive yelling for everyone to watch before he jumped. He was the one waving his arm dramatically before catching a pop fly on the softball field, yelling, "Mine, mine, I got it, I got it," even though no one was challenging him for the ball. He was the kid who played the loudest in band, yelled, "Yes!!" when he got his test paper back with an A on it, and always tried to make sure he was the center of attention wherever he was.

Today he's the guy who records his runs or workouts on Facebook, posts pictures of meals on Instagram, and tweets about his successes on Twitter. He's the one who drives the biggest car and lives in the biggest house, regardless of whether he can afford them or not.

Because of our dislike for the "Hey, Look at Me" kid, plus our natural inclination not to talk about ourselves, many people are loath to speak up and market themselves. They see self-promotion less as a tool to accomplish what they want and more as an opportunity to show off. But by using All About Them to generate marketing, public relations, and social media buzz, people can improve their businesses *and* get airline upgrades. The paradox of All About Them is that by concentrating on others, entrepreneurs and communicators can improve their own brands. This chapter concentrates on the simple steps to incorporating All About Them into your life and your business.

PLAYING THE NAME GAME

A few hundred years ago it was easy to know what someone did for a living. Mr. Shoemaker made shoes. Goldsmith hammered precious metals. Tailor sewed. Farmer farmed. Baker baked.

But it's not quite that simple today, is it? When was the last time you met someone named Dr. Radiologist? Mr. Hedge Fund Manager? Ms. Account Executive?

Does Jackson's father necessarily fix flats? Must Ms. Webman work on the Internet?

Of course not. Today we are free to pick the profession we think we're qualified for, regardless of the name we were born with.

So even though we can choose to be whatever we want, why is it we still use centuries' old nomenclature when we describe ourselves to others? Why is our first answer about ourselves a description of what we do for a living? And yes, I know you have a friend who knows a dentist named Dr. Payne or a lawyer named Ms. Lawless. My point still stands.

Picture this: You're at a party and meet someone new. You introduce yourselves, and the next thing out of your mouth is, "What do you do?"

If we still used the old system, being named for what we do, that question would be superfluous—last names such as Huntsman, Messenger, or Cook would tell our new friend exactly what we did for a living.

But the bigger question is why is our profession so important that "What do you do?" is the second thing we ask. Wouldn't it be more interesting, and more instructive, to ask, "Who are you," "What are you passionate about," or "What's important to you?"

Wouldn't we know more about our new acquaintance if we knew that he was an ardent hospice volunteer, collected eighteenth-century pastoral oils, or had recently emigrated from Perth rather than that he was a lawyer or an accountant? Wouldn't learning about this person's political leanings, religion, or taste in music give us more insight than being told his occupation?

In the past few chapters we've already seen that function is cost-of-entry when we market products or services. Just like the ante that gets us into a poker game, product function is a critical factor that allows us to sit down at the table, but it does not guarantee a successful evening or even a winning hand. Instead, how the product or service makes consumers' lives better—or makes consumers' perception of their lives better—determines success.

Up until now we've been talking about how the new realities we're all living in have conspired to change the way we need to think about presenting companies and products to the world. As we have seen, computerization, globalization, consolidation, and hyperfast communication have all changed the way we relate to one another and make decisions about the products and services we are going to buy and use.

But beyond products, services, companies, and organizations, these new realities also affect the way we need to think about ourselves and how we relate to others.

Just as no one will eat in a restaurant with sticky floors or bad food, if we're not good at our jobs, no one will hire us. At the same time being good at our jobs doesn't mean anyone will employ us. Why?

Because people don't choose what we do. They choose who we are.

THE DIFFERENCE BETWEEN FRONT OF THE HOUSE AND BACK OF THE HOUSE

There are two major areas of responsibility in a restaurant: the front of the house and the back of the house.

The front of the house mostly includes all the things you see: the lobby, the maître d', the bar, the dining room, and the servers.

The back of the house mostly includes all the things you don't see: the kitchen, the dishwashing area, the administrative office, refrigerated storage, wine and liquor storage, the garbage disposal area, and so on.

Knowing how the functions and responsibilities of a restaurant are divided, we shouldn't be surprised that both areas are critical to its success and that the best-run restaurants are those in which the front and back of the house work hand in hand.

It probably won't surprise you to know that many restaurants are home to long-standing turf wars where the maître d' in the front and the chef or manager in the back are constantly bickering and dickering over who is more important to the success of the eatery.

The folks up front think its popularity derives from atmosphere, the attentiveness of the service, the polish on the chandeliers, and so on; these, in their view, bring customers back time after time. Of course the folks in the back counter that the quality of the food, the freshness of the produce, the great selection of fine wines, and whatever else they handle generate repeat business. If the restaurant is large enough to have a business office and a marketing department or an outside PR firm (also back of the house), these entities will argue that the promos they create, the good press they generate, and quality reviews they develop get the word out and bring people in.

But after the diners have finished their meals and gone home, when the maître d' and the chef are relaxing at the bar, sipping their espressos or digestifs and rehashing their endless argument about who's more important to the restaurant, they always forget one factor.

The dishwashers.

You see, no matter how lovely the restaurant, and no matter how delicious the food, if dinner is served on dirty plates, longtime customers will leave and never return.

Think about that for a minute. You can enjoy a restaurant for years, celebrate meaningful family events there, and count on it for romantic dinners and special occasions. Then one day your plate arrives with an unidentifiable brownish crust on the rim, or an unidentifiable hair is tangled in the tines of your fork, and you never go back.

But here's the oddest part: while you've not returned to a restaurant because of dirty dishes (or some other sanitary slip up), you've never recommended a restaurant to a friend because of its immaculate plates and silverware. Have you ever exclaimed, "You'll *love* this place!! It has the cleanest dishes in town!!"

Clean dishes, just like all the other functional assets we've already talked about, are critical requirements for a restaurant to do business, but they are not the reason anyone does business with the restaurant. And crowing about clean dishes won't attract business either. At best, people will simply ignore that message; at worst, they will wonder why the eatery is bragging about its clean plates in the first place.

So if promoting the functional aspects of your business won't bring in customers, then what will?

EXPRESSING YOUR AUTHENTIC TRUTH

In his 2006 book *A Whole New Mind*, Daniel Pink explained that the way to assure business success is to create a compelling product persona that no one can copy. Pink's example? Madonna Louise Ciccone, popularly known simply as Madonna. According to Pink, Madonna has created the perfect business model. That's because people don't just buy what Madonna does—songwriting, singing, and dancing—they buy who she is: Madonna.

Of course it's important to remember that just as our world is in a state of flux, so is branding theory and practice. For example, while Pink was clear about a brand's need to develop an irreproducible product persona, he wrote *A Whole New Mind* years before Stefani Joanne Angelina Germanotta researched and repurposed Madonna's act and created Lady Gaga. And while she did not reproduce the Madonna persona itself, she did successfully sell an old persona to a brand-new market of pop music fans.

The other day I read a Twitter post that said, "OMG!! I just saw Madonna riding the subway." A few minutes later someone retweeted the comment with this reply: "That means Lady Gaga will ride the subway tomorrow, only not as well."

Instead of focusing on the things we do, we should concentrate on identifying who we are and why that resonates with

our current and potential customers. Because even though the
service we sell may provide the actual result they need, the relationship we build with them will entice them to do business
with us instead of our competitors.

People don't choose what you do. They choose who you
are.

THE DIFFERENCE BETWEEN YOUR MEDICINE CABINET AND YOUR MIRROR

Think about your medicine cabinet for a moment. In it are
all the lotions and potions, pills and powders that you use to
put your best face forward. If your medicine cabinet is anything like mine, the shelves are stocked with razor blades and
dental floss, outdated prescriptions and nearly empty bottles of
aspirin, some brushes and combs, and a few different brands
of cologne and aftershave—all the different concoctions and
gewgaws I use to get ready to face the day. I try to keep it neat
and organized, but truth be told my medicine cabinet is always
a little messier than I would like it to be.

Ah, but close the mirrored door and everything changes.
Because when you swing the cabinet door shut, you see your
face smiling back at you in the mirror. And if you're looking
at your reflection after you've used the cabinet's contents to
fluff and buff and primp and preen, then you are seeing the
best version of yourself.

That über-version, the idealized visage we create for special
moments, might not be possible without the content of the
medicine cabinet and its metaphorical partners—your hair-
dresser, your tailor, your trainer perhaps—but none of them

show up when you put your best foot forward. Instead it's the ten-tenths you that makes such a wonderful first impression.

BE YOURSELF, BE YOURSELF, BE YOURSELF

Books and articles written about the different times when looking good and having charisma is critical—job interviews, first dates, new client presentations—all recommend the same thing: be yourself, be yourself, be yourself. But it's that hyper-realized self in the medicine cabinet mirror, the best version of who you are, that sells the day.

Like an actor on the stage or an anchorperson on the news set, that practiced and prepared visage projects the confidence that tells audiences that you can deliver what they're looking for. It lets them know that they're making the right decision by putting their faith in you and what you're selling—be it a product, a service, or even a second date.

The problems occur in two distinct areas. First, our distaste for the "Hey, Look at Me" kid and our unwillingness to be like him makes actively selling ourselves difficult. Sure, we'll put a little extra effort into our appearance, but anything more seems phony and disingenuous and gets our defenses up.

Next, presenting an idealized self seems to fly in the face of our attempts to be real. On some level we feel that if we polish our images in pursuit of perfection, then we're not being authentic. Instead, we're marketing something other than our true selves, and that feels hypocritical. Be yourself, be yourself, be yourself, indeed.

That's where embracing the All About Them philosophy changes everything. Because you cannot create an idealized image that will build your brand and help you accomplish your goals in a vacuum. Such efforts simply create a self-centered brand persona that gets us dangerously close to the "Hey, Look at Me" kid's territory. In other words, instead of looking at the idealized brand as a false representation, you should create the new and improved version that is actually the truest version of yourself.

You want to build an idealized brand that speaks to your audience's needs and, more importantly, their wants. You want to build a brand that resonates with consumers and lets them know that their lives will be better because of your presence in them. You want to build an idealized brand that is you, only more so.

Whether you're a teen idol creating imaginary aspirational romances with hopeful high schoolers or a physician building a bond of trust and commitment with your patients, this idealized version of yourself—the hero from Campbell's "Hero's Journey"—fulfills the wants and desires of your audience. This construct works equally well for CEOs looking to develop a working rapport of loyalty and dedication with their employees, parents looking to build nurturing relationships with their children, and brand managers looking to attract repeat customers to their Internet businesses. This hyperrealized self, draws us toward the politicians we support, and its absence pushes us away. As we saw in the introduction, Barack Obama's "Yes we can" convinced over two-thirds of first-time voters to cast their ballots for the freshman Illinois senator in the 2008 presidential election against John McCain, a decorated war hero who had served two terms in the US House of Representatives and then moved to the US Senate in 1986.

While it would be nice to believe these young American voters chose Obama based strictly on the issues and were un-
swayed by more emotional concerns, cynical realism forces us
to accept that their decision reflected how the message resonated with them. "Yes we can" was positive, inclusive, and
aspirational, and represented the best of what the candidate
was offering—not just the best of himself but the best of what
the voters saw in themselves.

"Yes we can" was truly All About Them.

ALL ABOUT THEM IS ALL ABOUT PASSION

As discussed several pages ago, the All About Them way to
learn more about people and demonstrate your interest and
concern is to ask about their passions, not their professions.
When you do, you'll find that you unlock a vault jammed full
with excitement, commitment, and knowledge.

After all, while we all have different passions and hobbies,
we all look at them very similarly. That is, we all pursue our
passions with interest and enthusiasm and have acquired lots
of arcane knowledge that we're eager to impart (although not
many people around us may share our same curiosity about or
zeal for the subject).

But therein lies the fascinating truth—and the power—of
passions: we all care about different things, but we all do so in
much the same manner.

Years ago I tried my hand at autocrossing, the sport where
you race a car against the clock and other drivers' times, but
you're not on the track at the same time as your competitors. This allows you to use a moderately modified street car

without having to worry about damaging your automobile or yourself in an accident with another vehicle.

Even the suggestion that the event takes place on a track is a bit of a misnomer. Most autocrossing events are held in the enormous parking lots of airports, colleges and universities, shopping malls, ball parks, and other locations where big areas of asphalt can be safely roped off.

I drove a 1984 Porsche Carrera that I had prepared for the event by installing a roll bar and replacing the tires with a set made from softer compound rubber for better handling. Besides that, and my bright red helmet, my car—the same one I drove to work everyday, by the way—was pretty much exactly as it had come from the factory.

Of course, I still participated with all the zest of a Formula One grand prix champ. I walked around the paddocks and talked shop with the other autocrossers, enthusiastically comparing my car to the other machinery out there. Autocrossing Porsches was my passion.

One Saturday my wife came to an event and wandered around the pits with me, stopping to chat with the other "racers" I had gotten to know over the year or so that I participated. During one particularly long and jargon-filled conversation, another autocrosser and I discussed inflation rates, RSR accessories, suspension settings, model designations, and the like. Of course, my wife had no idea what we were talking about and was a bit exasperated. In frustration she turned to the girlfriend of the autocrosser I was chatting with and asked if she'd understood a word the two of us had said.

"Not a thing," the other woman answered. "I don't speak Porscheguese."

Coincidentally, the next day there was an orchid festival at Fairchild Tropical Gardens, and my wife—who loves gardening and orchids—asked if I'd go with her. While I care about orchids about as much as my wife cares about aging sports cars, I thought it was only fair that I return the favor, and so I went along.

The event was a huge celebration of the bright flowers. Hundreds of booths sold and displayed every strain of vanda, dendrobium, cattleya, and oncidium that you can imagine, as well as lots of exotic varieties that you can't. People in sandals and floppy hats walked in and out of the park with their arms full of potted plants, bags of special plant foods, and books on the proper care and feeding of orchids.

But I found most interesting the conversations in which orchid enthusiasts discussed their favorite flowers. They talked about "vulgar root structures," "proper hydration and vitamin supplements," and "optimal sunlight angles" with the exact same knowledge and fervor that my autocross buddies talked about "adhesive tire compounds," "oil viscosity," and "model designation variances." The object of the flower lovers' affections differed completely from that of the auto racers, but their emotional involvement was exactly the same. Both parties talked about their respective passions with the same intensity and ardor.

There's an old saying that generally refers to religious fanatics, political zealots, and fundamentalists of any stripe: "You can't logically talk someone out of something they didn't

logically talk themselves into." It eloquently explains the co-
nundrum of why facts don't override faith. Passion is a powerful force that can consume the person who experiences it.

Because of this, tapping into a person's passion is a powerful
All About Them way for brands to generate awareness, build
connection, and persuade consumers.

TRACKING PASSION

Most of us use some sort of contact management system across
our various digital devices—smartphone, tablet, laptop, and/
or desktop computer. And whether you use Microsoft Out-
look, Apple Mail, or a more powerful and specific customer
relationship manager (CRM) program such as ACT! or Sales-
force, the basic premise is the same. You fill out designated
slots with pertinent information, such as name, address, phone
number, and e-mail address. But while that information is critical, much like functional versus emotional benefits, it's not
enough to build a relationship on or further your cause.

Instead, knowing, understanding, and tracking your contacts' passions is the critical All About Them component that
will help you accomplish your goals.

Regardless of each program's sophistication level, most
CRM software allows you to easily create custom fields. While
people usually use these to track assistants' names and numbers
or contacts' ages and information about their children, why
not use them to track your contacts' passions? That will enable
you to make your correspondence and relationship with each
much more personal and intimate because you'll know what
the person you're communicating with cares about.

SMIRFS

Spelled with a *U*, SMURFS are cuddly blue cartoon characters who live in the Belgian forest in mushroom-shaped houses. Spelled with an *I*, SMIRFS is an acronym for the categories that encompass most people's passions. It's a great way for you to organize information about what others care about. SMIRFS stands for society, milieu, interest, religion, fraternity, and substance.

Society

Social connections can be a very real source of passion and interest. Knowing where people are from, what they were raised to value, and whom they feel connected to can be a great way to both understand them and demonstrate your specific affinity with them.

When I give a speech, for example, I always try to incorporate at least one Spanish word and one Yiddish word into my talk. That way, people in the audience who are societally attuned to these cues will notice and establish a slightly more intimate relationship with me. Conversely, people who don't speak those languages or are not familiar with the terms will skip right over them without notice.

In my case, the foreign words I use typically have to do with grandparents. For example, as I'm trying to illustrate a specific point, I'll mention my wife's grandmother and say something such as, "And so I checked to see if *Abuela* was sleeping." *Abuela* is Spanish for "grandmother," and Spanish-speakers in the audience notice my specific usage.

In a story about Nike and its tagline, I'll refer to my grandfather this way: "Just Do It reminds me of my Poppa Hi. I'd
say, 'I don't know Poppa, I don't think I'm going to do so well
on my algebra test,' and he'd tell me, 'It's all right, boychik,
just do it.' Or he'd ask me if I had a girlfriend, and I'd tell him
there was a girl I was interested in, but I was afraid to ask her
out. He'd tug on his goatee, smile at me, and say, 'What's a
handsome kid like you so worried about? Just call her up. Just
do it, boychik.'"

Boychik is a Yiddish diminutive term of endearment that
expresses the emotion of the moment, establishes my affection
for my grandfather, and lets the Jewish members of the audience know that I'm MOT (a member of the tribe).

Boychik and *abuela* make valuable connections between me
and my audience.

Milieu

Like society, milieu offers another great way to establish and
understand passions. Milieu, defined as "a person's social environment," is a great source of passion.

New Yorkers have a different milieu and environmental experience from Parisians, Los Angelinos, or Londoners. And just
knowing this can suggest the things New Yorkers care about.

But milieu is more than just geography. It can also encompass the political, educational, military, and other environments
that contribute to a person's self-description and interests.

You have to be careful, though, not to blindly assume that
milieu will accurately suggest a person's passion. For example, my friend and accountant Steve Demar and I went to the

University of Florida (UF) together. But while I have only a passing enthusiasm for the school's football team and its Florida Gators mascot, Steve is a died-in-the-wool crazy-eyed UF fanatic, a type of over-the-top fan commonly referred to as a "Bull Gator."

Recently I spoke about brand building at UF, and afterward my hosts gave me a beautiful bag full of Gator swag. There was a pen with an alligator-shaped clasp, an orange golf shirt with a big blue UF logo on the breast pocket, a UF baseball cap, and a leather business card holder with the UF logo embossed on its cover.

While I understand that regifting is usually frowned upon, when I gave the bag to Steve, he was as excited as a little kid getting his first tricycle on Christmas morning. Of course, nothing in the bag was expensive or valuable, and Steve could easily have purchased these things for himself. But that's not the point. Steve's milieu created a passion for the University of Florida that allowed me to create a great All About Them moment for him and me.

Interest

Interests, like Porsche autocrossing and orchids, are a great way to determine and utilize someone's passion.

One of my lifelong passions has always been music. From the age of six I was a rabid Beatles fan. From eight to thirteen I fidgeted through classical piano lessons. In junior and senior high school, my life revolved around the trumpet, and I spent most of my free time (and all of my skipped classes) in the band room or at concert band, jazz band, and orchestra rehearsals. I even went to band camp for two summers. Of course the bands I listened to were horn bands like Chicago Transit Authority, Blood, Sweat & Tears, and Chase.

In college I didn't have as much time for music, although I was a passable guitar player and enjoyed playing in bands, mostly as a way to meet girls. But after graduation, I was busy starting a business and a family and didn't find much time for making music.

Sometime around my thirtieth birthday, I was having a beer with my friend Rick and talking about music. Before becoming an advertising copywriter, Rick had been a professional trumpeter and had played with some of my favorite bands and performers, including Chicago and Marvin Gaye. Even though I had a fairly good understanding of music theory and classical and modern music history, Rick was shocked that I knew almost nothing about the blues—the root of jazz, rhythm and blues, and rock and roll. To counter my appalling lack of knowledge, Rick recorded two cassettes for me chock-full of classical blues music by Sonny Boy Williamson, Howlin' Wolf, Muddy Waters, Slim Harpo, Bessie Smith, and other greats.

It was a revelation! On these two tapes I heard everything that had attracted me in all sorts of music—syncopated rhythms, impassioned vocals, and buckets and buckets of raw emotion. The songs made me tap my feet and shake my butt and brought a huge smile to my face.

I also noticed that the songs I loved the most, those that really spoke to me, all had something in common. They all featured a harmonica (commonly referred to as a blues harp) wailing away.

A few years later, now a confirmed blues addict, I was in an airport waiting for a flight when I wandered through the gift shop and saw a thin book with a little red mesh bag clipped to it. The book was titled *The Klutz's Guide to Playing the Harmonica*, and the red bag held a diatonic harmonica and a cassette. I thought the little package would make a great gift for one of my kids. During a flight delay I pulled the book out and started reading. By the time we landed I couldn't wait to get into my car and listen to the instructional cassette.

Like so many activities (golf, baking, painting), playing the harmonica is really easy to do poorly and really hard to do well. As the late great harmonica teacher Bob Shatkin said, the key to playing the blues harp well is to "get such a shrill little instrument to sound as heavy as a freight train."

I read *The Klutz's Guide* over and over and listened to the accompanying recording every time I was driving. And even though my car had a manual transmission and I had to keep one hand on the gear shift, I practiced my blues harp everywhere I went. I even took private lessons and cycled through a few different teachers until I found one I could really learn from.

Now, twenty years later, I don't go anywhere without at least one harmonica in my pocket or a set of six or twelve in my briefcase. Whenever I find musicians playing on street corners for spare change, I pull out one of my harps and ask if I can join in. Thanks to my little harmonica, I've played with a violinist in the London Tube, a jazz combo in a town square in Provence, an accordion player in Berlin, and even another harmonica player in the Paris subway. He spoke no English, and my French was even worse, but we were still able to communicate and share our favorite riffs. At clubs and parties all around the country, I've played with famous and not so famous bands—I even got up on stage with José Feliciano in Las Vegas. And I've made lots of wonderful friends all over the world with whom I play music, e-mail MP3 files, and exchange links to articles about great harmonica players.

Because my business involves making presentations on an almost weekly basis, I've found that my harmonica playing is a great way to break the ice when I'm up in front of people. Blowing on my little blues harp lets the audience know that I'm not going to subject them to the same old presentation full of corporate blah blah blah. My music proves that I practice what I preach about the importance of creative differentiation in *Building Brand Value: Seven Simple Steps to Profitable Communications* (the title of my third book). It lets my audiences know that I don't take myself too seriously. I find that my renditions of Bach's Minuet in G and Sonny Boy Williamson's "Peachy Tree" are usually the most memorable parts of my time on the dais.

My passion for the harmonica has become such an integral part of my personal brand that I hand out harmonicas silkscreened with my logo and e-mail address as unique business cards, and people send me signed harmonicas as gifts. But most importantly, I still listen to great harmonica players, practice, and play my harmonica as often as I can.

Religion

Like society, milieu, and interest, religion provides a great opening for understanding people and what they care about.

But like sex and politics, religion is also often considered a subject to avoid in conversation and discussion so as not to give offense. Still, knowing people's religious beliefs can go a long way toward helping you understand who they are and what they care about.

Understand that my point here is not that you should make judgments based on people's faith. Rather, you should understand the importance that many people place on their religion (or lack thereof) as well as how their beliefs affect how they think and what they value.

In addition to being a source of passion in its own right, religion can also guide people to other passions that stem from their knowledge of, commitment to, and experience with their faith.

Fraternity

My wife's grandmother used to say, "Dime con quién tu andas y te diré quién eres." The English translation is "Tell me who you are with, and I'll tell you who you are." A more common English saying is, of course, "Birds of a feather flock together." Regardless of language, the meaning is clear: fraternal connections are a great way to determine people's interests and passions.

This is proven by the strength of teams, platoons, bands, or any group of people with a common connection, a common goal, or a common interest. By appealing to the sense of solidarity that groups of like-minded people create, brands can build powerful emotional bonds with consumers that enhance loyalty, stimulate sales, and even overcome the negative effects of brand crisis in the press or on social media.

It's no surprise then that ardent adapters and fervent followers of a particular product share the same sense of excitement and loyalty as other more recognized collections of people do for their causes. Many are so enthusiastic that they even self-identify with the person or object of their affections.

Rabid followers of pop star Justin Bieber are known as Beliebers." Grateful Dead followers are "Dead Heads." Taylor Swift fans are "Swifties." Beyonce has her "Bey Hive," and Jimmy Buffett has his "Parrot Heads."

And it's not just pop stars whose fans have self-identifying nicknames. Fanatical *Star Trek* viewers are "Trekkies." Evangelical users of Apple products are called "Fanboys." Alfa Romeo fans are "Alfisti." Travelers and linguists who favor France are "Francophiles." And as we've already seen, devotees of Porsche sports cars are said to speak "Porschegeuse."

Tapping into fraternal references like these is a great way to connect with consumers because organizing these enthusiasts around your brand gives them a way to both enjoy the connection and evangelize by bringing additional fans into the fold to build the fervor.

While the harmonica is my interest and passion, your passion is probably something very different. You may collect early-American quilts, play tennis, scuba dive, write poetry, or study Civil War battle strategies. Personal passions are as different as the people who pursue them. And so we need a classification for people whose random enthusiasms don't necessarily fit into the specific categories we've already identified.

Substance

Substance is the catchall category for the meaningful connections that don't fit under society, milieu, interest, religion, or fraternity. Because people's enthusiasms are as varied as people themselves, new and significant ways of categorizing people pop up just as quickly as new technologies make it possible.

What's more, people can fit into different categories based on different interests or how they express their passions. As the sixteenth-century essayist Michel Montaigne wrote about his own wandering mind, "I cannot keep my subject still. It goes along befuddled and staggering, with a natural drunkenness."

It doesn't matter which category you place people's passions in, however; it matters that you pay attention to them. After all, that focus is where you'll find emotional connection.

Throughout this book we've been talking about how to move the spotlight from you and your brand and focus it squarely on your current and potential customers. But when it comes to passion, there's a strong argument to be made for expressing your own commitment to an interest too. Sometimes to make it All About Them, you have to make it all about you.

PUTTING THE DOG AND PONY INTO THE DOG AND PONY SHOW

When advertising agencies pursue new accounts, the process often includes a creative presentation. Often called dog and pony shows in the trade, these are the agency's opportunity to show off its abilities. Of course, the best agencies design and stage these extravaganzas like Broadway productions, crafting each component of the show to best effect.

Robb High, a leading client-acquisition consultant, explains that while most agencies think new business presentations are about the speculative work they've prepared for the potential client, that's not their primary purpose. Instead, agency presentations serve more like first dates, giving the potential client some idea of what it will be like to work with the agency.

Knowing this, our advertising agency always tries to create its presentations and leave-behind pitch books in such a way that potential clients get to know us a little more than they might if we had only presented our businesses assets and attributes.

Besides talking about our services and highlighting our experience, our business materials include pictures and descriptions of everyone who will work on the new clients' business. And because of the importance we place on SMIRFS, our pitch books also include entertaining information about our professionals' personal passions.

Because of this, our resume pages don't just list our career and educational experience; they also include pictures and descriptions of us doing the things we love the most. My partner, Roberto Schaps, talks about his affection for travel and fine wine. Two of our art directors explain their love for bicycle racing; one is into road bikes, while the other loves trail riding and BMX. My bio expounds on my love for music and the bands I play in. And our public relations director talks about her love of fashion and trend watching.

THE SONS OF THE DESERT

A few years ago we were in the agency review for a major media company. Our pitch materials for this specific contest included a biography and photograph of our media director, a brilliant expert named Henry. Besides his knowledge of advertising distribution, Henry was also a big fan of the classic comedians Stan Laurel and Oliver Hardy. Henry was such a fan that he was the president of the local Miami Laurel and Hardy fan club, called the Sons of the Desert (the organization took its name from a lodge the comedians belonged to in a 1933 film of the same name). Of course we thought that talking about Henry's involvement with the Miami tent ("tent" is the organization's word for a local chapter of the group) would be a wonderful way to present him to our new clients.

But Henry was mortified. He protested that most people thought his hobby was stupid and that both his wife and daughter were extremely embarrassed by his participation—especially when he wore his bright red Sons of the Desert fez on his way to meetings. Needless to say, we didn't agree and finally convinced Henry to give us some pictures of his tent, officially called the Going Bye-Bye! Tent (Oasis 56), for inclusion in our agency leave-behind brochure.

During the actual presentation I was up in front of the eight people the client had brought. I was deep into my explanation of the strategic direction we wanted to take the client's marketing in, and I was just about to unveil the new campaign tagline when a big guy in a dark suit interrupted me.

"Hey! What's all this Laurel and Hardy stuff here in your brochure?" their president asked, waving our opened leave-behind over his head. "Who is this Henry guy?"

I started to explain that Henry was our media director and the president of the local Sons of the Desert tent. As I said so, I motioned toward Henry and looked his way. Our media director was staring back at me with eyes as big as saucers. Henry was white as a sheet.

"Well come on outside and tell me about the fan club, Henry," the president bellowed, gesturing toward the door of the conference room as he got up from the conference table. "My team can watch the rest of the presentation. I want to know more about this desert thing you do. I freaking love Laurel and Hardy."

Henry walked outside with the president, and they spent the rest of our presentation in the hallway talking about classic comedy films and whatever else Laurel and Hardy fans talk about when they get together. Needless to say, Henry made a great impression on the president even though he never got to present his media plan or even talk media strategy with our potential client.

While Henry hadn't demonstrated his knowledge and professional abilities, he had presented his passion and made an emotional connection with our potential new client. And in the end the relationship that Henry's passion encouraged proved much more valuable than another demonstration of another advertising agency's media-planning capabilities would have been.

Of course we got lucky that the president had the same arcane fascination with Laurel and Hardy as our media director.

But if it's true that you make your own luck, then it's also true that we never would have known about the president's interest or been able to exploit it to our advantage if we hadn't gone out on a limb and expressed our own passions in the first place.

The moral of this story is simple: whatever your overwhelming hobby or concentration is, make it an important and public part of your life. Share your interests, search out like-minded people, and incorporate your passion into your everyday personal and professional activities. You'll find that sharing your passion will make you more interesting, more approachable, and more memorable. Your passion—and your wholehearted expression of it—will serve as a magnet that draws people to you because of both their own like-minded interests and the attraction and excitement of enthusiasm. Sharing your passion will make you more human.

But even more importantly, sharing your passion will help eliminate any concern that you may have about blowing your own horn and shamelessly marketing yourself. In other words, sharing your passion will keep you from being the "Hey, Look at Me" kid, because when you share your passion with the world, you pivot from making the conversation all about you to giving a gift to those around you—turning them on to the knowledge, talents, and enthusiasms that both define you and can make their lives better. Sharing your passion helps you move from CC 2 CC (company centric to consumer centric) and makes your personal brand All About Them.

6

BEHAVING IN THE WORLD
OF ALL ABOUT THEM

THE DIVORCE ATTORNEY

A couple in their eighties made an appointment to meet with a divorce attorney. They told her that after discussing the ups and downs of their marriage, they both wanted to file for divorce.

The attorney was shocked. "How long have you been married?" she asked.

"Fifty-eight years," they answered in unison.

"And how long have you been unhappy with your marriage and wanted to separate?" the attorney queried.

"Forty years," the husband answered.

"It's been at least forty-five," the wife added.

"So why in the world did you wait so long?" the attorney asked.

The old woman answered, "We were waiting for the children to die."

THE GREATEST GENERATION

Tom Brokaw wrote the book about the generation of Americans who grew up during the Great Depression and fought in World War II. In his preface, Brokaw portrays the people he researched and wrote about as the saviors of humanity.

Brokaw is so impressed with this generation and its exploits that he calls them—and his book about them—the Greatest Generation. He spends his time interviewing its members and telling their stories and draws conclusions about their bravery, their sacrifices, their accomplishments, and the consequences of their actions.

Brokaw doesn't talk about how the generations that came after his greatest one—the baby boomers, Generations X and Y, the Millennials, and so forth—differed significantly from the Greatest Generation, especially when it comes to consumerism and branding.

While World War II was certainly not the last war in which generations of young Americans fought and died, it was the last to be fought by members of all levels of American society. And while too many American lives were lost in wars from Korea and Vietnam to Somalia, Afghanistan, and Iraq, World War II was the last to envelope and define an entire generation, regardless of social standing, financial wherewithal, or educational attainment.

As such, the generations that have followed Brokaw's greatest one have looked for new ways to define themselves, and many have embraced consumerism as their comprehensive, albeit shallow, defining factor.

For those of us born after the Greatest Generation, our lack of a defining moment in world history has forced us to look elsewhere. Rather than a war and the sacrifices demanded, we use the things we own and display to the world to define ourselves. Put simply, our parents' generation is known for the wars they fought; our generation is known for the things we bought.

SHORTCUTS TO UNDERSTANDING

The large black plastic keys for Mercedes-Benzes, BMWs, and Jaguars; the doorstop-shaped profile of the Toyota Prius; the bitten-Apple logo glowing on computers and phones; Ralph Lauren's polo ponies and Gucci's interlocking Gs—these are all icons that today's undefined generations use to tell the world who they are. Somehow Rosie the Riveter's "We can do it" has morphed to a multigenerational "We can buy it."

Even younger consumers who claim to eschew brands and commercialism use the things they own, from flip-flops to ironic T-shirts, and the things they display—tattoos and piercings—to establish their place in their own tribes of crunchies, hipsters, geeks, and more.

As discussed many times throughout this book, brands are defined not by the things their products or services do (their function) but by the emotional connections they make with consumers and the identifying properties they loan to those consumers.

In other words, good brands make you feel good. Great brands make you feel good about yourself.

GREAT BRANDS MAKE YOU FEEL
GOOD ABOUT YOURSELF

My running buddy David and I were at the gym talking about a trail race we had run in the Everglades. He was congratulating me on my performance when I pointed out how much better his time was than mine.

"It was a great race," David said. "You and I did the same thing."

"What are you talking about? You ran 50K to my 25 and your time per mile was faster than mine," I answered.

"No, we did exactly the same thing. We both went out there and ran the course as fast as we could."

This reminded me of the conversation between a Victorian worker and his liege:

> The rich man to the poor man, "If you'd bow to the king you wouldn't have to live with so little."
>
> Poor man to the rich man: "If you learned to live with less you wouldn't have to bow to the king."

Often the only thing that stands between success and failure—or the feeling of them—is how you frame the situation.

If you can stand another running story, let me tell you about my friend Adam.

Adam has been training as hard as I've ever seen anyone train—up before 5 a.m. to run grueling repeats around the track. He gets there so early and works so hard that he's often finishing his workout when I get there. By the way, in case you think Adam actually has the free time to train this hard, in his spare time Adam runs a Fortune 500 corporation and is a terrific father, husband, and community crusader.

When Adam went to run his big relay at the national championships, I couldn't wait to hear what happened. I saw him toweling off at the track a week later.

"How'd you do?" I asked.

"Let me tell you what happened in Kansas City," Adam said dejectedly. "One of our guys didn't show up for the race so we couldn't field a team in our 50–59 age group. We found another runner to take his place but he was in his forties, so we had to drop down to the 40–49 group."

"So how'd you do?" I asked.

"Well, we won the 40–49 division but there was no other team in it. If we had run in the 50–59 age group, we would have come in third."

"You won? You won the national championship? Wow! Adam, you won in a lower age group where the qualifying times are even more demanding. That's amazing."

"Nah, not really. I mean, yeah, technically we won. . . . But we didn't really win. It wasn't what we trained for."

Do you see what just happened? Adam took months of training, overcoming the loss of a team member, and winning a national championship and wrote it all off simply because it didn't happen the way he wanted it to happen—even though the last time I checked, the officials at national qualifying race events don't give out trophies unless you actually win fair and square.

Before you judge Adam too harshly, think about the last time you did the same thing.

Maybe you returned a compliment about how nice you looked with a disparaging, "Me? No, no, no, my hair looks terrible . . . and I need to lose at least twenty pounds."

Perhaps you blew off congratulations for landing a new job or winning a piece of new business by crediting it to having known the right person or been in the right place at the right time.

Or maybe you wrote off a smart investment or business decision to just being lucky.

Why are we so willing to beat ourselves up for the things we've done badly or haven't done at all, yet so loathe to take credit for the things we've actually achieved?

You see this in marketing all the time when companies build their branding programs around their weaknesses. They enumerate the items that they think will make their customers think they're big or accomplished or credible instead of talking about what matters most to their clients.

But savvy marketers don't talk about themselves. Instead, like the best of friends, they focus on the things they can do to help their clients overcome their own negative feelings.

And like friends, good brands make people feel good. But great brands make people feel good about themselves.

From the Greatest Generation to the best brands, the secret is providing not just a great product or service but the means for customers to internalize what you offer and use that brand identification to tell the world who they are and why they matter.

HOW TO BUILD CONNECTIONS WITH CONSUMERS

As we've seen, the best way to build brand value is to create an All About Them brand that your consumers self-identify with and even use to tell the rest of the world who they are and why they matter. From Justin Bieber's "Beliebers" to Barry Manilow's "Fanilows," such connection creates long-lasting relationships.

One study, financed in part by Samsung, investigated how consumers' identification with a brand's attractiveness affected the value of the brand asset. Researchers found that the positive relationship established between a brand and its consumers had a measurably important effect on a users' affinity with the brand and subsequent brand loyalty.

The twentieth-century solution to the consumer-identification problem was to create visible brand uniforms that users could wear proudly to proclaim their loyalties to the world—in much the way that the uniforms of British soldiers during the American Revolution declared their loyalty to the Crown and led to the nickname "Redcoat." This type of brand connection was an unsophisticated yet ubiquitous technique for consumers to easily broadcast their belonging.

Nike's swoosh and Adidas's triple stripes served the same purpose as Mercedes-Benz's stand-up hood ornament and Louis Vuitton's interlocking initials. No corporate golf event was complete without attendees sporting a series of impressive logos on their polo shirts, baseball caps, and backpacks. Things got so bad—and conspicuous brand consumption became so widespread—that by the turn of this century more than one company built a brand based on its lack of brand identification.

Using the tagline "When your own initials are enough," Italian fashion house Bottega Veneta played up its conscious lack of visible branding. It sold this counterintuitive idea with the sly suggestion that the people in the know would still recognize the brand, thanks to its quality. Moreover, those who didn't know what they were looking at lacked the proper social standing to matter. Of course, even though the designer espoused silent messaging, Bottega Veneta's leather products were still identifiable by the company's signature *intrecciato* weave (hand woven strips of leather), much as Burberry products could be picked out of a lineup by their exclusive tartan plaid, even if they didn't display a logo either.

Belgian fashion designer Martin Margiela, too, looked to create a "brand-free" aesthetic that didn't overexpose the company's provenance. But even this company, which prized itself on allowing users to respond to its products' style and "not just the idea of a brand expressed via a label," used a trademark stitching pattern and a plain, unmarked, white label or a cryptic but still identifiable label bearing the numbers zero to twenty-three to set its products apart from the crowd.

But as users of the latest digital technology say, "That's so five minutes ago." Today a brand's standing is easy to determine thanks to the utter transparency of democratized digital media. What's more, thanks to the ever-growing inventory of counterfeit products available online and overseas, a gold Rolex crown on a beautiful watch or a Ferrari prancing horse on a pair of red suede driving shoes no longer serves as proof that a product is genuine.

Today when it's becoming too difficult and too expensive for brands to police the proper use of their trademarks on a corporate level, it's crucial to create an evangelical horde of users who care about authenticity and will defend the brand themselves. Today it is necessary for brand communications to move from company centric to consumer centric (CC 2 CC).

CC 2 CC: MOVING FROM COMPANY CENTRIC TO CONSUMER CENTRIC

I was getting ready to make a presentation at a Fortune 100 company's annual innovation summit, and the person responsible for the conference program asked me, "What is the first word you think your friends/significant other/parents/siblings would use to describe your personal brand?"

I didn't have to ponder this at all, so my quick answer was, "Creative." After all, I was always the kid in art class, writing classes, band and orchestra, and rock bands. I have art and design degrees, for Pete's sake. "Creative" was the perfect single word to describe the personal brand I think I have.

But before I e-mailed her my answer, I remembered an experience that opened my eyes to a whole different personal brand descriptor that might be more accurate.

A few years ago my office was thinking about adding nameplates to everyone's office doors so that when we took potential clients on tours around our agency, they'd get a chance to be introduced to everyone. Then someone wisely pointed out that no one would remember a bunch of names (Pam, Carolina, Allison, Marlisa, Tom, Tracy, José, and so forth). Instead they suggested we put one-word descriptors for each person on his or her office door.

We thought that besides making practical sense, the idea could be fun and might even start some interesting conversations with our potential clients.

In our Friday breakfast meeting, we told everyone about the plan, and because we knew that people would agonize over their personal brand words, and because we wanted to get the words up right away, we asked everyone to please submit their words on the following Monday—or else a word would be picked for them.

Much smarter people than I have warned us to be careful what we wish for.

I was out of town the next week and never got around to submitting my own personal brand. When I returned to the office, the word art was already up. Our CFO's word was "thorough." One art director's word was "colorful." Our bookkeeper's word was "busy." Our tough-as-nails production manager's title was "The Hammer."

There was a word on my office door too. But oddly enough, it wasn't "creative."

Over the last pages we've been talking about your company's need to incorporate a CC 2 CC mind-set as you build your brand. In other words, forward-thinking organizations just like yours need to shift away from a company-centric branding strategy to messaging that's consumer centric. Because in today's interactive environment—where anyone can speak to everyone—you no longer decide what your personal brand is: your customers make and promote that decision.

Just as my officemates and I had completely different ideas about what personal descriptor word would best represent me, your customers also look at you, your company, and your products and services very differently than you do. If you don't know what they think, then you don't know how to market to or satisfy them.

Oh yeah, what was the word I found on my door? "Intense." Intense? Me? Go figure.

BEING OPEN TO CHANGE

One of the great assignments I've been lucky enough to work on was creating brands and marketing solutions for different Bacardi products.

We built programs to introduce and sell the company's goods to its various audiences, each with different wants and needs, tastes and desires. We developed Bacardi Black Magic to introduce Bacardi's dark rum (mixed with cranberry juice) to sophisticated drinkers in hotel bars. We created Bacardi Lite and Diet Coke ("only 66 calories") and promoted it to women in their thirties and forties who were both weight and taste conscious. We developed the Bacardi Gecko for Mexican-themed bars that were selling more tequila and less rum and the Bacardi Bat Bite as a seasonal Halloween specialty. But the campaign we had the most fun with—and learned the most from—was the Bacardi Cherry Bomb.

Our creative brief was simple: to find out what would motivate the legal-drinking age (LDA) audience in college bars to switch their drink of choice from beer to rum, specifically Bacardi dark rum. Bacardi chose this particular product because it had absolutely no market share in college communities, and so any new business would make a significant showing on the company's sales tallies.

Of course, we started our work with research. After all, the only way to move a brand from CC 2 CC, or from bragging about itself (company centric) to resonating with its customers (consumer centric), is to understand who the consumers are and what they care about.

Here's some of what we found:

First, young drinkers like to talk sophisticated, but they drink "sweet." In common language instead of spirits jargon: they like to appear knowledgeable about alcoholic beverages but tend to order sweeter, less sophisticated cocktails.

When we investigated why that was so, we found that most younger drinkers had started drinking with beverages they already understood and liked. That meant that their drinks of choice were usually Rum & Cokes or Screwdrivers because they knew and enjoyed cola and orange juice and felt comfortable ordering them, albeit now with an adult additive: alcohol.

We also found that while young drinkers primarily ordered alcohol to get drunk, their reasons for drinking, particularly among males, were more nuanced that that. LDA males told us that they drank to "get loaded and get lucky." And if they weren't going to get lucky, then that was even more reason to get loaded.

Based on this information, we developed a branded bar product called the Bacardi Cherry Bomb. Thanks to a mixture of Bacardi Black and Cherry Coke, the drink was sweet enough to make your teeth hurt after one sip. But of course we knew this would only please our target audience. To reach them, in-bar sales were encouraged with a series of posters and a fun interactive drinking ritual called "Slam it. Slug it. Slap it." The "Slam it" was an invitation to rap the square shot glass that the drink was served in on the bar. "Slug it" was the command to throw back the drink. And "Slap it" referred to a custom-made temporary tattoo that showed the special shot glass with a bright red cherry bomb inside. Of course the cherry bomb's wick was lit and sparkling. Finally, draped around the glass was a nautical-looking banner emblazoned with the name of the drink: Bacardi Cherry Bomb.

But it wasn't the specific marketing of that drink that proved so illustrative and such a great All About Them lesson for me. Instead my experience of presenting our concept to Bacardi's marketing team taught me the most.

Here's what happened:

I was standing in one of Bacardi's smaller conference rooms getting ready to present both the findings of our research and our subsequent solutions. The room was set up like a classroom and held about twenty people, all the team members for the product group we were working for. All were in their late twenties or early thirties and charged with selling Bacardi products to the LDA consumer group. Like you, they knew we were looking to understand the stimuli that the LDA cohort would respond to and to create a drink and promotion that would increase both product sampling and sales.

We started the presentation by showing photos of the different bars we visited around the country. Then we showed pictures of a random sampling of the different people we spoke with during our visits.

Next we scrolled through a number of charts showing the demographics (e.g., age, income, sex, level of education) of both the people we talked to and the specific audience targets that Bacardi had given us. I was about to go into some of the more specific input we had received when the back door of the conference room opened and a man slipped silently into the room.

All heads in the audience turned almost as one to see who had joined us. The man was middle-aged but in very good shape. His longish hair was perfectly combed, and he wore a beautiful sport coat tailored in a delicate, light green and cream houndstooth, a color combination I had only seen in Europe. The fabric would not have been out of place in the interior of the most expensive Mercedes-Benz.

I didn't recognize the guy, but he was clearly important. He stood in the back of the room with a quiet confidence and told me, "Please proceed, don't mind me." Not knowing what else to do, I went on with my presentation. Everyone in the seats before me turned back to face the front of the room.

The man stood quietly in the back as I went through all the facts and figures of our research. Eventually we got to the section titled "Consumer Motivation." With this slide projected on the screen, I started to explain why the consumers actually purchased the product and what was important to them. I also explained that the brand's traditional selling points—tradition, quality, provenance, and so forth—barely made it into their consideration set. "In fact," I went on, "our young consumers only seem to care about these attributes of the brand when they're looking for bragging rights. Remember we already saw that these are consumers who like to 'talk sophisticated,' but 'drink sweet.'"

"Excuse me," the guest in the back of the room interrupted. "But our brand has not been created for people who want to 'drink sweet,' as you say. It is created for people with discerning palates who want to savor the finer things in life." The man described how his grandfather had journeyed from Cuba with his special recipe secretly sewn into his lapel. He gave us a brief history of the family's exile on the island of

Puerto Rico and how they had labored for years to create the finest rum products available anywhere in the world.

Apparently I was talking to a Bacardi!

He went on to eloquently relate a bit more of his family's history and accomplishments, making it clear that he was not happy with the way his products were now being portrayed. Everyone else in the audience just stared at him raptly with respect or fear—I wasn't sure which.

Finally, our guest was done with his lecture, and it was my turn to talk.

"With all due respect, sir, when was the last time you bought Bacardi rum?" I asked.

"What? I always drink Bacardi rum," he answered, not unkindly but perhaps a little surprised. "What would you expect I would drink?"

"I'm sorry, but I didn't ask when you last drank Bacardi; I asked when you last bought it. And I don't mean when you slip a bartender your American Express corporate card and buy Bacardi for everyone in the bar as a sampling promotion."

He just stared at me so I continued.

"When was the last time you had only $20 in your pocket to last the entire weekend and your friend told you to bring a bottle of rum to the party? At the liquor store you could buy a bottle of Bacardi for $18 or Old Mr. Boston for only $12."

"Old Mr. Boston?" he interrupted, "*Pero qué mierda*, how can you compare that to our products?"

"I'm sorry," I apologized again. "I wasn't suggesting the two products themselves were actually comparable. I was only trying to point out that a college student with not much money in their pocket might have different purchasing motivations than you do. The truth is that students have significantly different purchase motivations from every single person in this room. And it's students' propensity to purchase your products that we were hired to both understand and stimulate."

"I see," Mr. Bacardi said. "Now that you've put it that way, I have to admit I've never had that experience. I've never actually paid for our products out of my own pocket, and I've never really worried about how much something cost or how much money I'd have left. I don't have any idea why that kid would buy our rum. Please proceed."

Turning back to my presentation, I explained the rest of the thinking that went into our brand creation work and then showed our creative solutions. When I was done, our guest walked to the front of the room, thanked me for the input, shook my hand, and went about his day.

Although he left the room quickly, our guest left me with a greater understanding of just how important it is to build brands with a thorough understanding of the anticipated consumers' mind-set. His willingness to put aside his own opinions, experiences, and prejudices—regardless of how important and deeply held they were—and open himself completely to someone else's viewpoint was a real eye opener. Even though I had been in the front of the room, the man in the back had taught the most valuable lesson.

IF YOU GET PAST THE BS, MAYBE YOU'LL FIND THE BULL

There's an old story about a pessimist father who wanted to teach his optimist son a lesson. The only thing the kid wanted for his birthday was a pony. So on the son's birthday, while the kid was away at school, his dad called the local feed store and had his son's bedroom filled with manure from floor to ceiling.

When the kid got home, his dad told him that his present was in his room. The kid could already smell the manure and squealed, "Oh goodie, you got me a pony!" as he ran toward his room.

A moment later the kid went streaking by in the opposite direction. He dashed into the garage, grabbed a shovel, and came running back toward his bedroom.

"Whoa there. Where you going with that shovel, son?" the father asked.

"With all that crap in my room," the boy answered as he ran past, "there's got to be a pony in there somewhere."

I was reminded of that joke the other day when my friend David Park sent me his notes from a Silicon Valley investors' conference. As he put it, "These words actually came out of human beings' mouths":

"We're swimming in the social stream."
"Crowdsourcing app discovery platform."
"Can you talk about getting conceptual liftoff?"
"Now let's talk about disrupting the disruptors."
"We're iterating our butts off, dude."
"Looks like it's searching for a substantiated use case."
"We're all about *glocal* right now."
"Collaborative consumption is truly a revolution."
"Plat-ag" (short for "platform-agnostic").
"You did one of the great pivots of all time."
"We don't measure our success by financial results."

Can you believe all this jargony hogwash? And this from our best and brightest, the IT geniuses who are busy creating the companies and opportunities that will energize the economy and produce tomorrow's millionaires and billionaires.

Jargon has always served to separate the in-crowd from everyone else. By using specialized insider language, people signal their inclusion in a given group or potentially alienate themselves from another.

Our presidential elections have become full of that sort of thing. Politicians and pundits use "code words" to let members of their base know they're talking to them when the messages they want to convey are less than politic. And sometimes a simple bit of ethnic slang, such as President Barack Obama's saying, "Nah, we straight," to a woman behind a restaurant counter, can effectively signal to certain groups that the speaker is "one of them."

But such conversational gymnastics can also backfire. Bill Clinton's "I'm fixin' to tell you" was a folksy, southern expression that spoke intimately to some but ran the risk of alienating more urbane voters. And while Paul Ryan's exaltation of Ayn Rand's writings signaled Tea Party conservatives that he was closely aligned with their economic beliefs, it also frightened religious conservatives who knew that Rand was an avowed atheist and lifelong supporter of abortion rights.

People make decisions based on their emotions and justify those decisions with their intellect. Often, not *what* you say but *how* you say it has the most emotional effect. That's what you need to keep in mind when you look to appeal to your customers' emotions before their intellects. And properly used, jargon and insider language can do that because they speak directly to the heart.

But remember that there might not be a pony under all that manure after all.

THE POWER (AND DANGER) OF JARGON

I have a confession to make: a few months ago I forgot to pay a bill. I've got no excuse for the oversight; I just didn't see the statement when I sat down to do my monthlies, and it completely slipped my mind. Hopefully we know each other well enough by now that you won't judge me too harshly. Let's just move on with the story.

I didn't recognize the number on my cellphone, but I answered it anyway. By the third word out of the customer service rep's mouth, I knew she had no idea who I was because she pronounced my last name "TUR-kle" instead of "Tur-KELL," the way anyone who knows me says it.

"Hello, Bruce TUR-kle?"

"Yes."

"This is Samantha Smith, customer service representative at XYZ Bank" (beautiful southern accent, by the way).

"Yes?"

"Your account didn't post."

"I'm sorry?"

"Your account didn't post."

"I don't understand."

"Your account didn't post."

"I don't know what that means."

"YOUR ACCOUNT DIDN'T POST." (She was a decibel short of yelling now.)

"I heard you, Ms. Smith. I just don't understand what you're saying."

"It means your account at XYZ Bank. Did. Not. Post."

"I'm really sorry, but I don't know what 'post' means. I know about blog posts, I know about light posts, I know about post times, and I know about Post cereals. I even know about post mortems. But I don't know what it means when an account doesn't post."

"Oh. It means we didn't post a payment to your account."

"You didn't post a . . . Oh, you mean my payment's late? Oops, I probably forgot to pay it. Wait, I'll look . . . [a few keyboard clicks later] You're right. I didn't pay my bill. That was stupid of me. Why didn't you just say so? I'll take care of it immediately."

"Thank you, sir. Is there anything else XYZ Bank customer service can do for you today?"

I bit my tongue. "No thanks. Appreciate the customer service reminder. I'll take care of it the minute I hang up." And I did.

Have you ever been in a tense medical situation and spoken to a doctor who communicated in medical jargon you didn't understand? Asymmetric thoracic reflux, perhaps, or cardiotropic defibrillation?

Have you ever met with your accountant to discuss taxes and been flummoxed by negative amortization schedules and accelerated deduction contra accounts or other industry terms that made no sense? Have you ever listened to people talk in slang or use inside jokes you couldn't follow? Have you ever been with people who were speaking a language you didn't understand even though you were supposed to be part of the conversation?

It would make sense for customer service people—who already have the difficult task of dealing with angry clients or explaining abstruse software or reminding people they didn't pay their bills on time—to make everyone's life easier by speaking in simple terms that anyone can follow.

If you're not convinced yet, try this illustrative experiment. Do an English-language crossword puzzle from a country foreign to you. Even simple puzzles are almost impossible to complete, because while American English might be your mother tongue, because you didn't grow up in Canada or England or New Zealand or India, you can understand the words of their crossword puzzles but not necessarily the cultural references or the clues. It's no different for a customer who can understand the language but not the insider jargon the customer service rep uses.

I actually learned this a few years ago from our creative director, Soren Thielemann, who grew up in Denmark and moved to the United States sometime after college. Because he was from northern Europe, Soren was fluent in Danish, German, and English, and although he poo-pooed his abilities, he spoke good Spanish and French as well.

Soren was telling me a story about an international advertising agency he had worked for in Europe and how it would send him to different countries to edit television commercials. Most of northern Europe was his territory, and the agency sent him to Sweden, Norway, and Holland, among other places.

"How could you edit commercials in Norway?" I asked incredulously. "Do you speak Norwegian?"

"Not really," Soren answered. "But I kind of can if I have to."

"Do you speak Swedish?"

"No. But I sort of understand it."

I'd go on through the list of the countries and languages Soren had told me he had worked in, and his answer was always the same. He didn't really speak the language, but he could still get by.

So imagine my surprise when the whole creative department was at lunch one day, and Soren stopped our conversation with the words, "I have no idea what you're talking about."

I was stunned that someone fluent in at least three to five languages, able to speak a handful of other languages well enough to turn out professional work, and as naturally fluent in English as you or I couldn't understand what we were chatting about.

It turned out that even though Soren understood the words we were saying, he didn't understand the cultural references or the jargon we were using to make our points. From sports statistics and abbreviations to television references to movie lines and song lyrics, the native-born among us were speaking in a specific culture as much as we were speaking in a specific language. Whether referring to a *Saturday Night Live* skit from childhood or a political reference from American history, our group was using information that simultaneously brought us together while it kept others out.

Interestingly enough, both of those observations are important to creating effective All About Them language.

Understanding your audience's cultural upbringing and influences means you can better communicate with these consumers to create instant rapport and deeper understanding.

Referring to things that matter to your audience and to you (remember the connection forged through a mutual enthusiasm for Laurel and Hardy discussed in the last chapter?) is a great way to demonstrate concern and affinity and establish an intimacy that builds connection and consensus.

BILL O'REILLY, THE TRUEST BRAND IN THE WORLD

Cultural references and properly used jargon build a "one-of-us" intimacy that can create strong customer loyalty. And when combined with a brand's authentic expression of self, this connection becomes even stronger. Perhaps the best way to illustrate this point is with a clear example of a brand that is congruent with its owner's authentic self and its clients' desires and uses a powerful cultural language to establish and maintain the connection.

Throughout this book we've talked about a number of powerfully congruent brands. A strong list would include names we've mentioned and others we haven't—Apple, Porsche, BMW, Panerai, Ralph Lauren, Harley-Davidson, Prius, Las Vegas, Miami, and Hermès.

But perhaps the truest brand example I can think of to make this point is Bill O'Reilly. Seriously. Bill O'Reilly.

Before I explain, let me issue a prophylactic disclaimer. I'm neither condoning nor condemning O'Reilly's politics here. For the sake of illustrating the concept of true brand value, I've gone out of my way to be as personally, professionally, and politically agnostic as possible. The point here is not to comment on the what but to understand the how. You might love O'Reilly or you might loathe him (there doesn't seem to be much middle ground between the two poles). But regardless of your personal opinion, please put it aside and look at O'Reilly as an example of a well-formed combination of strategically spoken cultural language, clearly expressed authentic truth, and carefully constructed audience connection.

I was a guest on *The O'Reilly Factor* almost two years ago. The show's producers wanted two marketing experts for O'Reilly to interview about ESPN's decision not to run a Christmas-themed television commercial for a Catholic children's hospital. Coincidentally I was invited to be on the show alongside a friend, tech/social media genius Peter Shankman.

O'Reilly contended that ESPN's refusal to run the spot was a clear example of what he called "America's War on Christmas." And if O'Reilly had actually allowed me to explain why ESPN had disallowed the commercial, I would have told him about three factors.

First, in order not to offend viewers, ESPN—like all television networks—has policies regarding how much religiosity it will allow. Before you jump to conclusions, look at it this way: most Americans won't mind Christian messages, and many will accept Jewish messages. Fewer still will tolerate exposure to Muslim doctrines on their TV set. But how about Baha'i teachings? Or Wiccan sermons? Or even proclamations of Pastafarianism (the Church of the Flying Spaghetti Monster)? Because these are all accepted religions, guaranteed freedom of expression under the Bill of Rights, the network's choice is to limit all or to limit none. And so it has opted for the former.

Second, EPSN—like all television networks—has clear charity requirements. I don't know for sure, but I would bet that the potential advertiser didn't fill out the required 501(c)3 forms; therefore the network couldn't be sure that any money donated would be used appropriately. If the advertiser failed to fill out the forms and then misused the money, the network could be held accountable for abetting fraud. To quote YouTube sensation Kimberly "Sweet Brown" Wilkins, "Ain't nobody got time for that."

Finally, if you watch the spot you'll see that the little boy in the commercial is wearing a surgical mask. And you might notice that the mask has a big red splotch on it. Ick, right? Understandably, no TV station wants its viewers changing the channel to avoid looking at blood.

O'Reilly, one of the highest-paid personalities on television, knows these things better than I do. But explaining them to his viewers neither promotes his brand nor engages his audience.

O'Reilly has strategically built an aspirational brand by living the life his viewers wish they could. He targets disaffected, formerly middle-class, general-market consumers who are angry that rampant technology, increased minority rights, painful economic realities, and encroaching old age are eroding the lifestyles they once enjoyed. And so O'Reilly brilliantly fabricates crises, such as "The War on Christmas," to empathize with his audience. He whips his viewers into a frenzy by first enraging them, then offering the catharsis of manhandling his guests. Quite simply, O'Reilly beats up his mostly affluent, well-dressed, well-educated, and/or minority guests because his audience wants to pummel them themselves but cannot.

By doing this, O'Reilly has perfectly aligned his authentic self with his audience's deepest desires. He has also created one of the truest and most profitable brands on television.

Admirable? Maybe not.

Illustrative and replicable? Absolutely.

All you have to do is remove O'Reilly's signature rancor, and you'll see there's a lot to learn from and emulate in his brand, regardless of how you feel about his politics, practices, or policies.

Communicating in the clear, unambiguous language your audience speaks is a simple way to create a powerful connection with your customers. And expressing your authentic truth as their aspirational reality strengthens this connection even more.

Of course O'Reilly is hardly the only person or company to use negative reinforcement to create an All About Them relationship with consumers. Fear, as it turns out, has long been a go-to source of connection and control.

THE PROFITABLE BUSINESS OF FEAR

The Australian company SAMS has been working to create a new wetsuit design to lessen the fear of shark attacks.

SAMS (an acronym for Shark Attack Mitigation Systems) says it has optimized its designs to effectively cloak surfers. The company hired scientists who explained that sharks are monochromats and therefore color-blind. So researchers chose patterns they believed would both camouflage the wearer and also repel the sharks.

If that didn't provide enough protection, the designers also worked with the theory that sharks don't like to eat sea snakes, and so they created designs that looked like them—a questionable strategy, however, because the scientists admit to having only anecdotal evidence of the claim. What's more, sharks also focus on their potential victims with their lateral line, a collection of sensory receptors running laterally along their bodies, and can discern the vibrations their prey generate.

All this work makes me wonder why protecting divers from sharks is such an important issue in the first place. After all, while the prospect of a shark attack is certainly terrifying, such attacks account for only four or five deaths a year—worldwide.

Four or five deaths across the entire planet—that's less than for almost any other cause you can imagine.

In 2012 alone, 7.4 million people around the world died from heart disease, 6.7 million died from stroke, and 1.5 million died from diabetes. Based on these numbers, one has to wonder why there is so much interest and investment in a cause of death that kills only four to five people a year.

More interesting to me than whether or not the designs will work is the question of their marketability. After all, SAMS is not investing all its money out of a desire to keep people safe from shark attacks; they're hoping to profit from people's fear of being killed in one.

Okay, so maybe you don't dive. Maybe the closest you've come to a shark is peering through aquarium glass or watching *Finding Nemo*. Why should you care? Because marketers and politicians are using statistically unwarranted fear to sell goods and services to you too.

As horrible and frightening as terrorism and assaults are, for example, they kill a relatively limited number of people in the United States for the amount of press they receive and fear they generate.

Worse, potential attack scenarios have become the go-to issue for politicians hoping to capture the hearts and minds—and contributions and votes—of a populace consumed by fear.

Pharmaceutical companies also use certain diseases and medical conditions to sell their wares, despite the fact that the conditions they protect against can be better dealt with through meaningful lifestyle changes such as improving diet and increasing exercise.

But marketers don't just exploit the fear of death. Even a tagline as seemingly innocuous as FedEx's "Absolutely, Positively Overnight" tapped into the fear of missing a deadline. Miss Clairol's "Does She or Doesn't She?" played on women's anxiety about being caught coloring their hair. Both the "Heartbreak of Psoriasis" and "Never Let Them See You Sweat" preyed on our fear of being embarrassed by our bodies. Even Viagra's mandatory, albeit seldom read, disclaimer, "If you have an erection that lasts longer than four hours," can be seen as marketing fear—in this case fear of the painful condition known as priapism (although I must say I think it's actually a not-so-subtle boast about the product's efficacy).

Products sell not because of what they can do but because of how they make consumers feel. And while one would think that good feelings would sell more products, the amount of fear-based marketing suggests just the opposite.

Every four years you'll see a host of presidential candidates using statistically unwarranted fear to attract your attention and interest and get you to vote for them. I fear they've churned up enough blood in the water that it's getting harder and harder to figure out who the dangerous sharks really are. And it will take education and awareness—not just a SAMS suit—to keep us all safe from their attacks.

Like a dangerous scent that sends a herd of gazelles leaping through the high grass of the African savanna or a loud noise that startles a flock of starlings off a power line, assertions that provoke fear can motivate a large group of voters to do what a candidate or lobbyist wants; they can also motivate consumers to do what manufacturers and advertisers desire as well.

But whether brand communications enhance consumers' good feelings about themselves and connection with the brand or prey on voters' anxieties and fears, they are an effective and oft-used method for creating cohesion and motivating outcomes. The question is, which method would you rather employ to create your own formidable brand identity?

The next chapter shows you how to do this in the most powerful—and positive—way possible.

7

MOVING INTO ALL ABOUT THEM

THE RATTLESNAKE

A little girl was walking down a frosty forest path when she heard a cry for help.

Not seeing anyone nearby, she finally looked down and saw a rattlesnake coiled on the ground near her. The snake looked up at her plaintively and hissed a barely audible, "Help me."

"Help you?" asked the little girl. "Why would I help you? You're a nasty, poisonous rattlesnake. All you want to do is bite me."

"No," hissed the snake. "I'm a magic rattlesnake. If you save me, I'll grant you whatever wishes you want. It's freezing out here, and I'm cold-blooded. If I don't warm up soon, I'm surely going to die."

"How can I save you?" asked the little girl.

"Just zip me up inside your jacket," hissed the snake. "Your body temperature will warm me up, and I'll be able to grant your wishes. And you don't have to worry about my biting you because if I were

stupid enough to do that, then your body would get cold, and I'd freeze to death."

The little girl did as she was told. She picked up the frozen serpent and slid it inside her sweater, zipping up her jacket to keep out the bitter wind. The frozen snake was icy cold against her warm skin.

After a few minutes the little girl felt the snake start to wiggle about. Before long it had warmed up enough that it started coiling around her waist. The snake's movements tickled, and the little girl started giggling.

A moment later the little girl felt a sharp pain in her side. She unzipped her jacket, lifted her sweater, and found the snake with his fangs sunk deep into the soft flesh between her ribs.

"What have you done?" the little girl asked in horror. "You promised you wouldn't bite me. Now I'm going to die, and when I do, I'll turn icy cold, and you'll freeze to death. Why would you do that?"

"Why are you surprised?" the snake answered. "You knew what I was when you picked me up."

YOUR AUTHENTIC TRUTH IS HIDDEN IN PLAIN SIGHT TOO

A host of realities have unwittingly conspired to change the world we live in so quickly, so profoundly, and so comprehensively that many of us are still wandering around wondering why our old habits no longer work. As we've seen, a lot of the old techniques that once assured personal and professional success simply don't pay off anymore.

Thanks to the Great Recession, many companies are not replacing the bloated bureaucracies they used to require. If you were a well-paid middle manager and got laid off, you're probably finding that the jobs you used to interview for are nowhere to be found.

Thanks to technology, many companies can produce products of market-acceptable quality regardless of where they are in the world. If you've been selling your products based on how they function or how good they are, you now understand why your sales are slipping or have fallen off completely.

Thanks to the ubiquitous reach of the Internet and faster and faster delivery services, consumers can buy whatever they want from wherever and whomever they want. If you're a bricks-and-mortar business that relies on foot traffic, you might be waking up to the new reality that your customers are using you as a hands-on showroom before they purchase online.

If you've experienced any of these situations, you're probably wondering what to do to build—or rebuild—the business you want. It is becoming clearer that today's consumer is looking for ways to find authenticity and real passion in a world full of digitally homogenized pablum. As we've said, the answer can be found in the simple reality that while a good brand makes people feel good, a great brand makes them feel good about themselves. Consumers want brands that deliver what they promise while also delivering a good dose of positive experience.

In the case of brand phenomenon Harley-Davidson, Senior Vice President and Chief Marketing Officer Mark-Hans Richer told the *New York Times* this about the iconic motorcycle's first electric vehicle: "To be a true Harley . . . it has to be cool. It has to make you feel something important about yourself." When asked about the technical descriptions,

Richer added, "We're not getting into spec wars at this time. The point is how you feel riding it."

The way to create this feeling is to deliver the true essence of what your business provides. The core of Harley's brand is not a trumped-up, overhyped, generic facsimile manufactured to be all things to all people but a carefully crafted expression of the company's simple truth fashioned in leather, rubber, and chrome. Harley's customers want the same thing people want from the artisans at their local farmers' market, the engineers at Tesla, the musicians in the E-Street Band, the chefs in that exciting new food truck, the software engineers at Adobe, the athletes on the US soccer team, the pilots in the Blue Angels, and, yes, the gear heads at Harley-Davidson. People want the truth.

If it's just another generic product, consumers may or may not work harder to get it, may or may not spend more to buy it, and probably won't pursue it if it's not readily available online. But products or services like the ones above often cost more and require consumers to work harder to obtain (walk down an alley, wait in a line, get on a waiting list).

Lucky for you, your brand's authentic truth is already there. Like the rising sun you might have enjoyed this morning, your truth already exists, hidden in plain sight. You just have to figure out how to uncover and develop it. The rest is easy.

IS VOLKSWAGEN'S AUTHENTIC TRUTH AN ASSET OR A LIABILITY?

By now everyone on the planet knows about Volkswagen's troubles. Quite simply, Volkswagen knowingly and maliciously installed software in its "smart diesel" cars designed to provide false emissions readings to government testers around the world. Estimates are that Volkswagen's diesel engines pollute at levels forty times greater than US government regulations allow—that's not twice or even three times as bad but forty times worse.

If you think that Volkswagen is screwed right up the ol' *fahrvergnügen*, you're right. At the time of this writing, the company had already lost over $18 billion, and that's probably just the tip of the iceberg. But don't count the world's biggest car company out. Because if every cloud has a silver lining, then Volkswagen could turn this fiasco into a great opportunity too.

First, let's look at why this is such a problem for Volkswagen. After all, Toyota, Audi, GM, Honda, and others have all suffered disastrous public relation gaffes and come back strong. But this time it's different. Because while those other companies' issues were bone-headed mistakes, Volkswagen's incorrect pollution readings were not caused by an error— the company knowingly misled the regulators. This was not an accidental flub; it was a deliberately perpetrated crime.

In a perfect world, Volkswagen would be the perfect company to push its smart diesel technology. The brand's authentic truth had been built and confirmed across years of happy little vehicles like the Beetle, the Bug, the Microbus, the Rabbit, the Golf, and the Eos. Volkswagens were warm, fuzzy, friendly, and trustworthy. Clearly Volkswagen's admission of guilt violates this trust.

Worse, Volkswagen drivers who were deceived feel particularly wronged because they thought they were saving the world. Now that they see that their emperor has no clothes, they know that they've actually been poisoning the atmosphere, pumping forty times more pollutants into the heavens than they thought.

So how can this possibly be good for Volkswagen?

Once the smoke clears and Volkswagen has cleaned house and fixed its immediate problem, the company has the opportunity to do something huge. Instead of just slinking into the corner and hoping no one remembers its crimes (a very likely scenario, by the way, considering consumers' short memories), Volkswagen could marshal its considerable resources of money, engineers, and multinational facilities to take the leadership role in the green revolution and dedicate itself to truly creating environmentally safe automobiles.

Besides saving the company, this strategy would also help Volkswagen, colloquially known as "Germany Inc.," save face for its entire country.

Of course, proper brand strategy promoting this new authentic truth would be an important part of the company's rebirth. But before that can work, Volkswagen has to commit itself to following a new path that will not only help undo the damage already done but also reengage customers and build a new sense of pride and purpose for the company, the country, and fans around the world, instead of just applying a marketing Band-Aid to the wound.

It won't be cheap, it won't be quick, and it won't be easy. But this type of brand-aid will provide Volkswagen with an opportunity not only to earn worldwide forgiveness but to take off like a bat out of *schnell*.

Volkswagen's authentic truth made its problem considerably worse but can also become its salvation.

FINDING YOUR OWN AUTHENTIC TRUTH

In order to compete with other fast-food restaurants, Taco Bell introduced its Dollar Craving Menu—a list of eleven items that each cost $1. To help promote this new pricing, Taco Bell created its Everlasting Dollar campaign in which up to eleven winners could win the chain's food for life (or at least $10,000 worth) if they could find specially modified dollar bills with unique serial numbers in general circulation.

Although the odds of winning this promotion are estimated at 2.4 billion to one (you probably have more chance of being struck twice by lightning while winning your state's lottery than winning Taco Bell for life), the campaign was heavily promoted across social media and worked well for the company because it is intrinsically aligned with the brand's authentic truth.

You see, while you might think Taco Bell's business is about Mexican food, or at least fast Mexican food, that's no longer true. Taco Bell may trade fast Mexican food for money, but its true brand essence is all about filling customers' bellies for little bits of money—$1 at a time. That's its authentic truth.

TOM MONAGHAN IS NOT IN THE PIZZA BUSINESS

I almost never meet people on airplanes—I guess my headphones and open laptop discourage conversation. But my good friend Bob Berkowitz, CEO of Multivision Video, often meets important people on planes. He believes that his American Airlines upgrades are worth every penny because the person he sits next to in business class will invariably become a client.

A number of years ago Bob sat next to Tom Monaghan. Bob says when he realized his seatmate was the Domino's Pizza magnate, he turned to him and said, "I love your pizza. It's my favorite." Tom looked at him for a moment before politely disagreeing, pointing out that Domino's really wasn't Bob's favorite. Instead, he said, there was some little pizza parlor in Bob's neighborhood that served better pies. "Maybe you like their fresh mozzarella, or their crispy crust, or their meatballs, but there's something about their pizza you prefer," Tom said.

Now Bob is a lot of good things—an innovative businessman, brilliant networker, savvy tech mind, lightning-fast Morse code keypunch operator, great father and big brother, and all-around great guy—but he's no gourmand. Domino's might very well be Bob's favorite pizza after all. But Monaghan didn't know any of this and went on to explain,

> You see, we're not actually in the pizza business. We're in the "it's 7 p.m. on a school night, and I don't feel like cooking" business. We're in the "the guys just got here to watch the game and there's nothing in the fridge to eat" business. We're in the "the twins' birthday party is tomorrow, and I've been working all week and haven't had a moment to go to the store" business. Our pizza doesn't have to be the best. It has to be the best hot food you can easily get in thirty minutes or less.

Why else do you think we ran a thirty minutes or it's free promotion? If we take more than thirty minutes to deliver, you've got lots of other options: you can pop a frozen pizza in the oven; you can call a local pizza parlor; you can drive through another fast-food restaurant. But if you need to feed a crowd in thirty minutes or less, we're the best solution.

Who knew?

But if Tom Monaghan knows he's not in the pizza business, doesn't that make you wonder what business you're in? Pizza Hut did.

Pizza Hut thought that just because it was in the pizza restaurant business it could also be in the free pizza-delivery business, just like Domino's. But according to Wikipedia, back in 1999, after offering free delivery, Pizza Hut found it could add a fifty-cent delivery charge in its Dallas–Fort Worth restaurants. By the summer of 2001, it was charging fifty cents in 95 percent of its company-owned restaurants and a smaller number of its franchises. What's with that? If Domino's needed to promise "thirty minutes or it's free," how could Pizza Hut charge extra for delivery? Pizza Hut discovered that it was in a different business from Domino's, and its customers would pay extra for the extra service.

Domino's Pizza trades food for money too, but its authentic truth—what its tribe identifies with—is its promise to deliver an acceptable solution within thirty minutes. The problems the company solves? The kids are hungry; my friends came over to watch the game; it's late, and I don't feel like cooking;

we need more food for the birthday party. That's the business Domino's is in.

So what business are you in? What is your authentic truth that attracts business to you as it separates you from your competition?

As stated so many times already, people don't choose what you do; they choose who you are. What you do is the functional solution that customers might come looking for, and it is what you trade for money, but it's not why people do business with you and your company.

When you were in the market for a mortgage, how did you choose the people you did business with? If you provided the right amount of collateral and were willing to pay the going rate, you could get money from lots of banks, credit unions, finance companies, and more. So why do you decide to do business with one organization or another?

Let's say you're a public speaker and simply market yourself as such. Your business is all about getting up in front of big groups of people and both entertaining and educating them about your area of expertise. Your specific customers are the meeting planners, event coordinators, and speaker's bureau representatives who hire presenters for the different conventions they produce. In order to get these assignments, you write a great speech, prepare a compelling PowerPoint presentation, and practice, practice, practice until you're confident you can pull off a flawless performance. Then you create websites, brochures, and other marketing materials to tell your potential customers that if they've got fifty-five minutes or so to fill in their agendas, you're the best person for the job.

Sounds like a good strategy, right? Trouble is, there are thousands of other speakers who offer the same thing you're offering. Some are more expensive than you. Some are cheaper. Some are better. Some are worse. But a customer with only an hour or so on a conference agenda has a lot of choices for whom to hire. And sad to say, the odds that they'll pick you aren't very good, regardless of how entertaining, engaging, and erudite you are.

But if your potential customer wants Guy Kawasaki, or Bill Clinton, or the pilot who landed that plane in the Hudson River, or the world's leading expert in reconstructive surgery, or Melissa Francis from both *Little House on the Prairie* and FOX Business, then just any old speaker won't do. And neither will you.

So the real question is, How do you raise your brand equity to occupy that kind of space in your clients' mind?

One of the most important ways is to understand exactly what your customers are buying—and to recognize that it's not your function. Instead, they're looking for your authentic truth—the genuine, intrinsic, and irreproducible benefit you provide that they just cannot find anywhere else.

SO WHO THE HELL ARE YOU ANYWAY?

We've talked about function; we've talked about passion; we've talked about skill sets and knowledge and talents. We've even talked about how to be not only yourself but the hyper-realized version of yourself that the world is looking for.

But beyond those considerations, who the hell are you anyway?

American humorist Mark Twain said, "The two most important days in your life are the day you are born and the day you find out why." Understanding (and exploiting) your authentic truth comes directly from this same idea. Knowing who you are (or what your company is) is the key to understanding and promoting your authentic truth.

> Volvo = safety
> Bill Clinton = charisma
> FedEx = peace of mind
> Mother Teresa = compassion
> Harley Davidson = rugged individualism
> Martin Luther King = civil rights
> General Electric = innovation
> Gandhi = austere nonviolence
> Brunello Cucinelli = conservatory craftsmanship
> Albert Einstein = genius
> Nike = ultimate athletic performance
> Ronald Reagan = hope

If you were going to describe your company or yourself with just one or two words, what would they be?

NATURE ABHORS A VACUUM

Figuring out your own authentic truth and applying it to your messaging and your life may be difficult, but it is the key to building your brand value. Plus, only when you know exactly what you stand for can you begin to move your brand positioning from company centric to consumer centric (CC 2 CC) and channel that knowledge into a powerful marketing strategy.

But there's another important reason to do this work. It's the simple reality that your brand will be created whether you take responsibility for doing it or not.

Seen in this light, understanding your own authentic truth and creating your own All About Them brand is not just marketing frippery or even a First World problem. It is a crucial requirement of marketing yourself for success in today's interconnected world.

Of course, not everyone in the public eye has made this leap and defined him- or herself, even though one of the leading precepts of political marketing is that candidates must define themselves before the competition or the media does it for them.

Did you know that Al Gore never said, "I invented the Internet"? During an interview on CNN's *Late Edition with Wolf Blitzer*, Gore said, "During my service in the United States Congress I took the initiative in creating the Internet. I took the initiative in moving forward a whole range of initiatives that have proven to be important to our country's economic growth and environmental protection, improvements in our educational system."

You are free to interpret that statement as Gore's claiming responsibility, or you may choose to view it like the myth-busting site Snopes.com, in whose interpretation Gore "was not claiming that he 'invented' the Internet in the sense of having designed or implemented it, but rather that he was responsible, in an economic and legislative sense, for fostering the development [of] the technology that we now know as the Internet."

But regardless of what Gore actually said (or meant), and regardless of how you look at it, the damage was done: the common belief is that Gore said, "I invented the Internet." Why? Because perception is reality, and nature abhors a vacuum. If you haven't identified and promoted your self-definition, someone else will.

Did you know that Sarah Palin never said, "I can see Russia from my house"? Tina Fey actually made the quip famous on *Saturday Night Live* when she parodied the then vice presidential candidate. Palin did say that one could see Russia from her state, which is technically true, thanks to the narrowness of the Bering Sea and the closeness of the respective countries' land masses. But regardless of who actually said what, the damning silliness of the statement "I can see Russia from my house" hounded Palin throughout her short-lived national political career.

Legendary head coach Joe Paterno led the Penn State Nittany Lions from 1966 to 2011. In 2007 he was inducted into the College Football Hall of Fame, and in 2011 he won his 409th game, becoming the winningest coach in Division I college football history. To people who lived in University Park or attended Penn State, he was an icon of almost religious significance.

On November 4, 2011, a grand jury report accused Paterno's former defensive coordinator, Jerry Sandusky, of sexually abusing eight young boys. One month later the number of victims had climbed to ten. On June 22, 2012, Sandusky was found guilty of forty-five of forty-eight criminal counts, and on October 9, 2012, he was sentenced to thirty to sixty years in prison.

Just a few years later, the survey research firm Wilson Perkins Allen Opinion conducted a poll of over 1,000 adults. Surprisingly, only 55 percent of Americans questioned knew that Penn State head coach Joe Paterno had not been accused of molesting children; 45 percent believed that Paterno had been the attacker.

By this point, Paterno had already been removed from his post at Penn State and died of complications from lung cancer. But the truth didn't even matter posthumously. Perception is reality, and Paterno's legacy has been tarnished forever.

It's a common belief in the marketing world that "perception is reality"—that is, people's perceptions establish their reality. In a more practical sense, if we believe Starbucks coffee is better than the unlabeled stuff, then it is better—we will go out of our way to find Starbucks and pay more money for it, even though we really have little way of knowing if Starbucks' coffee actually is superior, or even different, from cheaper or less-known brands.

If we believe a Volvo is a safer automobile than the others we could drive, then it is—at least in the showroom. We will pay a higher price for the car because of its perceived value of enhanced protection. Of course, investigators establish whether the car is actually safer after an accident, but that occurs long after the product has been selected and purchased.

In 1897 Mark Twain published one of my favorite books, a travel guide titled *Following the Equator: A Journey Around the World*. In it he writes, "Truth is stranger than fiction, but it is because Fiction is obliged to stick to possibilities; Truth isn't."

Or as Lord Byron wrote in *Don Juan* some fifty years before Twain, "'Tis strange—but true; for truth is always strange; Stranger than fiction."

Truth might be stranger than fiction, but oftentimes fiction is more interesting, more exciting, more replicable, and ultimately more powerful and compelling than the truth. And those who don't embrace this reality of branding and perception do so at their own peril, because perception is reality.

Just ask Al Gore. Or Sarah Palin. Or Joe Paterno.

Once you've figured out who you are and what you stand for, the next logical step is to communicate that identity. But it should be clear by now that just broadcasting your message is neither a strategic nor effective All About Them way to relate to your audience. Instead we need to translate your message into a CC 2 CC communication that resonates with your intended market.

Besides that, it's equally important to communicate your message in a way that furthers your desire to build your brand and motivate your audience to action without wasting time telling them things they already know or don't care about. The way to do this is to transform their *needs* into *wants* and their *whys* to *hows*.

TURNING NEEDS INTO WANTS AND WHYS INTO HOWS

A number of years ago I tried to figure out why our ad agency wasn't quite as successful as I would have liked. After much soul-searching and teeth gnashing it finally dawned on me that we had been trying to sell something our clients might not be interested in buying.

Quite simply, we were trying to sell better design work, and they wanted to buy better sales. Sure, the situation was a bit more complicated than that, but boiled down, that was the gist of the disconnect.

Now I understand clearly that unlike the Medici family that hired Michelangelo to paint the ceiling of the Sistine Chapel, our clients are not patrons of the arts. Instead they look at what we do as a means to a very real end: increasing revenue. Of course we're perfectly welcome to get our jollies by crafting our branding creations anyway we'd like, but in the end we need to solve our clients' problems and sell their products.

Interestingly, as we evolve our business and continuously look for ways to reinvent what we do—using more and more sophisticated technology, more and more talented practitioners, more and more complicated programs—the core service we provide gets simpler and simpler.

In other words, it's our job to turn needs into wants and whys into hows.

Needs to Wants

You need a laptop computer to do your homework. You want an Apple MacBook.

You need a car to get to work in the morning. You want a BMW.

You need a sweater to keep warm. You want a Chanel sweater set.

You need a refrigerator to keep your food fresh. You want a Sub-Zero refrigerator.

You need a watch to tell the time. You want a Patek Philippe.

One of the biggest challenges presented to all of us by constantly evolving technology is the abundance of products and services it facilitates and the commoditization it creates. Products and services once exclusively produced by sophisticated companies and professionals within developed countries now glut the market because computers make it easy to produce and distribute them quickly and cheaply all around the globe. And whereas there used to be significant differences in quality between the goods produced by these different companies and countries, once again computers have closed those gaps.

So while being in a business where people buy products based on needs used to be a strong market position, it isn't anymore. If I live up north where it's cold, and I need to get warm, for example, many tropical beach destinations can solve my dilemma. But that creates a competitive situation among tropical destinations that drives vacation costs steadily downward. Good for the traveler perhaps, but not so good for the hotels and amusements that service them.

In the past, simply offering a warm beach vacation was enough to attract cold winter visitors from the north. Today that only works for the lowest-common-denominator tourist destination.

If you're going to an event and need a new pair of silver pumps to match your gown, most any brand that sells formal shoes can solve your dilemma. And if you're happy with the look, fit, and price, you won't care very much about which brand you buy. Of course we already know that function is

simply cost-of-entry and does not create brand loyalty, provide differentiation, or build brand value, and the astute reader
will notice that those three attributes all refer to the function of
the brand. Again, this dependence on needs (warmth or silver
pumps) invites competition and drives prices down.

But if you are fashion-forward and want a pair of Jimmy
Choo or Louboutin pumps, then their absolutely outrageous
prices will seem utterly acceptable and reasonable. After all,
if you *want* those shoes, you won't be satisfied with anything
else. And the high prices might even add to your desire because they suggest exclusivity, quality, and uniqueness, just
like the long wait to get a table at Joe's Stone Crab Restaurant
actually adds significant perceived value to the institution's appeal. It's the opposite of the old Yogi Berra line "Nobody goes
there anymore, it's too crowded."

What causes this? Consumer perception, otherwise known
as brand value. It's the perception of brand value that makes
an Apple iPad worth more than a no-name Korean tablet and
a cup of Starbucks coffee worth more than the same drink
poured at the corner diner. Are Apple's iPad and Starbucks'
venti half-caf cappuccino actually better? That depends on
what you need and how sophisticated your palette is. But the
distinction is ultimately irrelevant; the desire for the brand—
the want—makes the product more valuable.

Of course this sea change in manufacturing and the resultant
glut of acceptable goods on the market is a relatively new phenomenon. It used to be that being in a business where people
bought products based on needs was a strong enough market
position. When quality was rare—or at least expensive—good,
solid value and performance were the demand of the day, and

many companies built their brands and reputations on that sort of product delivery alone.

In 1980 Sears told the world it was where "America shops for value." It sold Craftsman tools guaranteed for life and Toughskin jeans guaranteed to hold up to anything your kid could dish out. But as it watched sales decline, Sears realized that there was more to selling products than simply bragging about their durability. To combat the decline, they embraced the 1990s with the "Softer Side of Sears" campaign, showing that it not only had products for both men and women but sold an entire line of fashion-oriented products, such as lingerie, notable for attributes beyond toughness and durability. Even its competitor Kmart hopped on the wagon, suggesting that people who shopped in its stores were savvier than other stores' customers with the tagline "There's smart, and there's Kmartsmart."

Unfortunately, neither campaign resonated with the companies' authentic truths, and neither company did very much to change the actual reality of the shopping experience it provided. While both talked a good game about building strong emotional connections with their consumers, nothing shoppers found in either store—from products to service—backed this promise up. By not aligning their messaging with their authentic truths, both companies significantly damaged their brand value. Sears lost its toughness imprimatur without replacing it with something more universally compelling, and Kmart lost its reputation for low prices while also not supplanting it with something stronger. To quote advertising icon David Ogilvy, "Nothing kills a bad product faster than good advertising."

But company sales can also benefit by understanding the difference between needs and wants. Pharmaceutical companies provide good examples of the market advantage to manipulating this distinction. After all, they benefit by selling branded medicinal products at much higher prices than their chemically identical generic versions. And often the expensive branded product and the generic bargain brands sit right next to one another on the pharmacy shelf. Some shoppers understand that the products are chemically—and therefore functionally—identical and opt for the less expensive choice, knowing it will have the same effect on their condition. But the fact that more than 80 percent of drugs sold are name brands demonstrates pretty clearly that more than three-quarters of all consumers are willing to pay extra money specifically for the brand name attached to the pill bottle. And this despite the empirical evidence that there is no difference in the products' efficacy. In other words, these consumers have been effectively moved from needs (the physical response to the medicinal compound) to wants (the emotional response to the brand). What's more, the continued sales of branded products suggest that consumers value the want over saving money.

Whys to Hows

If you build a successful brand, you move your consumer not only from needs to wants but also from whys to hows. You no longer have to spend your time, effort, and hard-earned marketing dollars convincing potential customers why they should use you. Instead you can focus your efforts on showing them how they can hire you. Doing this properly reduces the need for competitive pricing, filling out mind-numbing requests for proposals, and putting on expensive dog and pony shows for prospects. When clients want to hire you—not just someone who does what you do—you'll find that the entire sales cycle changes, and the hows become the meaningful explanations that will get you hired.

Needs to wants and whys to hows. It took me years and years of hard work and missed opportunities to realize that it couldn't be much simpler than that. So let's explore how to both align perceptions with reality and create the emotional bonding that builds strong brand relationships with your consumers.

THE PR SHOESHINE

Each time I get off the plane at San Juan's International Airport, my favorite PR shoeshine entrepreneur is there, waving crumpled passengers into his little polish parlor.

I'm so fond of the five minutes I spend in his chair that when I fly to Puerto Rico to visit my client, I even make a point of wearing shoes that need a bit of touching up. That way I get a good shine, I get to reward his entrepreneurship, and I look that much spiffier when I pull up to my client's office in Old San Juan.

But on my last trip, my PR shoeshine guy added something new to the experience and taught me a valuable lesson about how to expand services and revenue opportunities with very little additional work or marketing.

When my shoeshine was almost over, my shoeshine guy stuck out his hand, looked up at me, and asked, "¿Y su cinta?" ("And your belt?").

Without thinking, I unbuckled my belt, slid it from around my waist, and handed it to him. The shoeshine guy dabbed a little polish on it, gave it a good buffing, dried it with a noisy black blow drier, and handed it back to me, along with a bill for $7 more than I usually spend.

The best part? Not only did he double the money he made from me, but I thanked him for the extra service. It wasn't until I started writing about the experience that I realized that he had moved me from why to how. He didn't have to explain why I should have my belt shined. His question, "¿Y su cinta?" simply showed me how to better enjoy the five-minute shoeshine indulgence and how to look a little more put together.

Smart restaurant operators show they understand this concept when they look to add new items to their menus without adding additional inventory and cost. Chinese and Mexican restaurants can teach you a master class in creating new products from the same old ingredients while giving customers more reasons to come back and try new things.

Infopreneurs, too, are busy figuring out new ways to increase their offerings by repurposing their content across blogs, books, websites, video blogs, audio interviews, and more. To meet this need, software developers keep creating new apps such as Snapchat, Vine, and Periscope to take advantage of this phenomenon.

What opportunities does your business provide for increasing both customer satisfaction and revenue without much addition to your inventory or skillset? A quick look around—at both what you do and where you can move your customer from whys to hows—should provide you with a number of chances to grow your business. Ironically, you'll find that most of these opportunities are already there; you're just not availing yourself of them. In other words, they are hidden in plain sight.

HIDDEN IN PLAIN SIGHT

Ironically, asking your customers what else they'd like is not usually the best way to uncover the opportunities hiding in plain sight. When asked how much market research he had done for the iPad, Apple visionary Steve Jobs famously answered, "None. It's not the consumers' job to know what they want."

Instead, look for the problem that's not being solved, the itch that's not being scratched, the solution that's not being offered. Contrary to popular advice, you should try to answer the question that's not being asked because that's often where the gold is hiding.

You've already seen the proof. Although I get my shoes shined regularly and almost always wear a belt, it never dawned on me that my belt needed polishing too. That is until my favorite PR shoeshine guy suggested it to me. But the fact that I've never had another shoeshine guy make this offer or suggest cleaning and polishing my briefcase, for instance, makes the point.

And speaking of hidden in plain sight, when I started writing this chapter, I thought the "PR" in PR shoeshine stood for Puerto Rico. But now I realize that it could stand for public relations. Because what could make for better relations with your public than pleasing them with something they didn't know they wanted? And if it helps you make more money for very little additional expenditure, then PR can also stand for profitable revenue! Either way, it all comes from that simple pivot from needs to wants.

HIDDEN IN PLAIN SIGHT IS NOT MONKEY BUSINESS

I'd like you to watch a video on YouTube. In it you'll see two teams of kids playing with basketballs. One team is dressed in white, the other in black. While you watch the video, be very, very careful to keep track of how many times the white team passes the ball.

I know that when I provide a video link, there's a good chance you won't watch it. You figure that you'll just plow on through my words and get around to watching the video later if you're still interested. And anyway, you probably don't want to get up out of your warm, comfortable chair to turn on the computer. But please don't put this off. To really understand my point, please go to the link and watch the ninety-second video first. Remember your assignment is to carefully count how many times the white team passes the basketball.

Ready? Just copy or type this link into your web browser to watch: https://www.youtube.com/watch?v=vJG698U2Mvo/.

My very good friend, the late Joachim de Posada, author of *Don't Eat the Marshmallow—Yet!*, first turned me on to this video. I was so stunned by what I saw that, after Joachim's

presentation, I insisted that he run his PowerPoint again because I just couldn't believe what I had just seen (or didn't see,
to be more precise).

[*Spoiler alert:* If you haven't already gone to the link and
watched the video, do it now before you read any further.]

Did you count the turnovers? Do you know how many
times the team passed the ball back and forth? Are you sure?
Okay then, answer me this: Did you see the man in the gorilla
suit walk through the scene? It's hard to believe you could
miss a guy in a full, furry gorilla suit, isn't it?

Can you believe it? You were so busy counting the hand-
offs you didn't even see the big gorilla. And it's not like the
gorilla ran quickly through the scene; he even stopped and
pounded his chest right in the middle of the room. Go back
and click on the link again; you'll be amazed at what you see
this time.

The filmmakers call this phenomenon "The Invisible
Gorilla." Magicians call it misdirection. The best illusionists
make you look at their moving hand or their flourished scarf
while stealthily going about their tricky business elsewhere.
When you're trying to follow the pea the carnival grifter slides
back and forth under the walnut shells, you're the victim of
misdirection.

But could this happen in your everyday life too? Imagine
just how many things we miss each and every day because
we're so busy looking at something else.

Maybe we didn't see our kids smiling by our side because we
were too busy watching the big game. Maybe we didn't catch
the stunning sunset because we were too busy checking our text

messages. Perhaps we didn't enjoy what we have because we were too busy chasing whatever it is that we don't have.

Like the white arrow positioned smack dab in the middle of the FedEx logo, plenty of meaningful things are hidden in plain sight each and every day.

You've never seen the arrow? How can that be? You've seen that FedEx logo at least a million times. You've probably even seen it at least once today—on a truck near your office or on an envelope on your desk. And the arrow is right there—it's the negative white space between the *e* and the *x*. See it now?

THE EARTH SHATTERING MOVE FROM INTELLECT TO EMOTION

Much as slamming the door or kicking the tires reassures a prospective buyer of a vehicle's solidity, a strong brand provides a level of emotional satisfaction that helps create and build the relationship between your company and your consumer. The brand's power is to both reinforce and "preinforce" the consumer's decision, creating emotional bookends around the purchase experience.

You'll notice that the move from needs to wants and from whys to hows can best be described as a pivot from the actual to the emotional. When a brand, a company, a person, or an argument makes this move, it gains the advantage of significant brand value by changing the way consumers perceive and relate to it.

Think back to the conversation we had about Barack Obama's 2008 campaign results in Chapter 5. Perhaps you remember the staggering statistic that more than two-thirds of first-time voters cast their ballots for Obama. If you think about it logically, I think you'll agree that it is beyond the scope of reason to believe that all of these first-time voters were fully versed in the issues, had compared and contrasted the platforms and voting records of both candidates, and had made empirically sound decisions before they chose their president. No, there had to be something more.

As we have seen, Obama's campaign tagline, "Yes we can," was a powerful emotion bomb: it was positive (yes), inclusive (we), and aspirational (can). It specifically appealed to the emotions of an electorate that had grown tired of the old doom and gloom and wanted something new and compelling.

Ironically, Ronald Reagan used the same strategy to electrify the Republican electorate in 1980:

> I've spoken of the shining city all my political life, but I don't know if I ever quite communicated what I saw when I said it. But in my mind it was a tall proud city built on rocks stronger than oceans, wind-swept, God-blessed, and teeming with people of all kinds living in harmony and peace, a city with free ports that hummed with commerce and creativity, and if there had to be city walls, the walls had doors and the doors were open to anyone with the will and the heart to get here.

And if this weren't enough, Jesus Christ himself used a similarly positive, inclusive, and aspirational line in his Sermon on the Mount in Matthew 5:14: "You are the light of the world. A city that is set on a hill cannot be hidden."

Clearly a strategy for building strong relationships and in-spiring positive action that has stood the test of at least two millennia is a powerful one indeed. And when executed prop-erly, this pivot from intellectual to emotional can produce nothing short of magical results. And that's the secret behind All About Them.

8

THE HEART OF ALL ABOUT THEM:
UNDERSTANDING CC 2 CC

THE MENACE MANTRA

"The best thing you can do is to get very good at being you."
    —*Dennis the Menace*

THE ART AND BUSINESS OF SELLING TIES

My client was one of the best-dressed men I'd ever met. Frank's shirts and suits were always immaculate and precisely tailored to fit his lanky frame. His beard was perfectly trimmed, and he always got his accessories—tie, cufflinks, watch, shoes—just right.

So imagine my surprise when I walked into his company headquarters and found the head fashion buyer, Frank, sitting at a worktable behind three stacks of the ugliest ties I had ever seen. He greeted me with a quick nod of his chin, but his hands never stopped moving between the different piles.

Frank started with the long, corrugated box of ties laid out directly in front of him. He'd pull one tie off the top of the pile, hold it up to the light, and examine it closely for a quick moment. Then he'd either toss the tie onto the stack on his right or drop it into the much smaller group on his left, yank out another tie, and repeat the process.

While Frank worked his way through the piles, I tried to figure out what he was up to. Finally, I couldn't stand it anymore.

"What's up, Frank?" I asked. "I don't understand what you're doing."

"I'm choosing ties for the stores," he answered without pausing. "This box," Frank motioned with his eyes, "has the tie samples the mill sent for our consideration. These ties," he gestured left, "are the ones we're going to keep and sell. These," he gestured right, "are going back to the factory."

I looked at the three piles but still couldn't see any difference.

"But Frank," I finally asked in desperation. "All of these ties are ugly. You wouldn't wear any of them. How are you picking between them?"

What Frank told me next was a life changer.

"I'm not our customer, Bruce. If I only ordered ties that I like, we'd go out of business." He paused to drop another reject on his right. "None of these ties are wearing ties. They're selling ties. The important thing is to know the difference."

There's a difference between wearing ties and selling ties? Who knew?

My great-uncle Manny once put his money into onion futures. The way my mom explained the investment to me,

Manny bought a future interest in a boxcar of onions that hadn't been harvested yet. When it came time to sell the onions, he'd make money if prices were higher when the vegetables were ready for market than when he bought them.

Unfortunately, Manny wasn't a sophisticated investor, and he waited too long to sell his onion futures. One day he got a call from the train depot asking where he wanted his onions delivered.

Apparently Uncle Manny's selling onions turned into eating onions (and then rotting onions). Manny's investment got eaten up too.

A few years ago there was so much construction going on in my hometown that people said our official bird was the crane. Every newspaper and magazine in town crowed about Miami's condo boom or warned about a bubble. Then condo sales hit the fan, and the real estate business plummeted into the crapper. An estimated seven- to ten-year glut of empty condos now sat on the Miami market. But within the last two years, the surplus has sold, and the sky is again streaked with cranes.

But while all those condos sold, the buildings they're in are still dark at night because most of the properties were bought as secure places for off-shore investors to park their money, not raise their families.

Turns out there are also selling condos and living condos.

Of course the lesson is simple: if you're creating products or services for yourself instead of your customers, then you might be building wonderfully creative and functional products that no one wants to buy. And no matter how well you construct your products or how little you charge, if they've been created for a market of one, then they haven't been created for the market.

If you're in the business of creating beautifully crafted products for yourself, you're not a businessperson; you're an artist. And to steal a line from the movie industry, there's a reason why that trade is called "show business" and not "show art." Because just like there are wearing ties and selling ties, there are watching movies and selling movies.

Understanding the difference and how to take advantage of it is all about understanding the move from company centric to consumer centric (CC 2 CC).

EVERYTHING'S THE SAME

Walk around the Las Vegas Consumer Electronics Show, and one thing becomes very apparent: electronics manufacturers and distributors have fully embraced tablet computing.

Just a few years after Apple introduced its first iPad, every single company, it seems, has come out with a tablet. You can order them in any size you want, with different processing and memory capabilities, and in a rainbow of colors and designs. If you stand quietly and listen carefully, you can feel Adam Smith's concept of supply and demand at work as you hear the sound of prices dropping.

Why is it then that Apple's iPad is still the top seller in the category at prices significantly higher than the competition? Certainly not because it was first in the category. Microsoft gets those honors, having released its first tablet computer way back at the turn of the century, at least ten years before Apple's iPad.

My business partner, Roberto Schaps, got back from a restaurant show in Chicago. His quick report? Every manufacturer is selling the same thing: rows and rows of vendors selling knives; rows and rows of vendors selling cookware; and company after company—from originator Keurig to KitchenAid, Nespresso, Hamilton Beach, Mr. Coffee, Cuisinart, and more—selling coffee machines that work with those little prepackaged coffee capsules.

As we've seen, today's globalized, computerized, 24/7/365 manufacturing economy can produce anything consumers want—from coffee pods to tablet computers—in any style or quantity and in almost any quality or price range—a state of affairs driven by what *New York Times* columnist and author Thomas L. Friedman calls the "three largest forces on the planet—globalization, Moore's law and Mother Nature."

President Barack Obama confirmed this in 2016 in his final State of the Union address: "The economy has been changing in profound ways, changes that started long before the Great Recession hit and haven't let up. Today, technology doesn't just replace jobs on the assembly line, but any job where work can be automated. Companies in a global economy can locate anywhere, and face tougher competition."

So why would anyone buy one product over another?

Please don't be obdurate and roll out that old trope that the best product gets the nod. If that were true, we'd have all embraced Betamax video over VHS and Apple's original personal computers over PCs, and not a single boy band since the Jackson 5 would have ever sold a single song. Not one.

No, consumers are much more complex and nuanced than that. As Dale Carnegie put it, "When dealing with people, let us remember we are not dealing with creatures of logic. We are dealing with creatures of emotion." And creatures of emotion make decisions based on the warm-and-fuzzy way they feel about things, and they then justify those decisions with cold, hard facts.

Even customers who make their purchase decisions based on the bloodless choice of lowest price are still often making an emotional decision. While their budget realities may dictate low-price purchases, they still use their buying practices to tell the world who they are and pride themselves on having the acumen to find the best price and get the best deal. Think about how often you've complimented a friend on a garment or accessory only to be told how cheap it had been at Marshall's or TJ Maxx.

It's becoming more and more the case that companies can no longer depend on innovation and speed-to-market alone to reach their sales goals. Instead they must develop and cultivate a powerful brand that entices and nurtures the kinds of loyal consumers who will return time and time again to buy their products. And while company after company comes out with tablets of every shape and size, Apple's rabid fanboys will still line up for each new iPad release because they have to have not just its improved functionality but the brand halo ownership bestows on them.

Of course, functionality is critical. After all, the days of people lining up to buy beautiful but fragile Ferraris and Maseratis are long gone—today the cars are as reliable as they are beautiful. But in a world of bumper-to-bumper traffic, radar-controlled speed limits, and intersections monitored by cameras, it should be clear that those cars continue to sell out for reasons that have little to do with their ability to get their affluent owners from point A to point B. Each auto's brand

and what it says about the driver, not its function, fuels continued record sales. And while manufacturers must never stop innovating lest they lose their competitive advantage, they must never stop developing their brands and cultivating their audiences lest their buyers go elsewhere.

So where do we find the solution?

THE BIGGER THEY ARE, THE HARDER THEY FALL

When production and profits were based on physical assets, it was common knowledge that large enterprise drove business. After all, if you owned the railroad, as the robber barons of the nineteenth and twentieth centuries did, you controlled the movement of raw materials and goods. If you owned the telegraph and telephone cables or the radio and television transmitting technology—as the largest telecommunications companies and media conglomerates did—you controlled the conversation. But as we've discussed, democratized communication and globalized ubiquity have shifted that paradigm and moved the locus of power from ownership to innovativeness.

Today, the bigger the company, the less likely unmanaged marketing messages are to result in a comprehensive, cogent, and ultimately valuable brand. Today it is crucial that all communicators within a company understand what their brand is and how it should be communicated to the company's various publics.

The old-world method of accomplishing this was a brand standards manual that showed marketers and designers specifically how they could reproduce the company's image (e.g., logos, typefaces, colors) to mechanically maintain a comprehensive image.

But in today's increasingly transparent world, companies must make sure that their messages are not only aesthetically accurate but also communicate across all channels, including popular social media sites—even those yet to be created. And a clear, All About Them, CC 2 CC strategy that speaks directly to customers' hearts is the way to do that.

WILLY WALKER FIGURED IT OUT

In May 2015, I was invited to Amelia Island, a beautiful resort just northeast of Jacksonville, Florida. Walker & Dunlop (W&D) had asked me to address the annual get-together of its most successful producers and significant clients.

Founded in 1937, Walker & Dunlop says it is "one of the largest providers of commercial real estate financing solutions." The company originates loans for sale to Fannie Mae, Freddie Mac, and the US Department of Housing and Urban Development. It also brokers loans to life insurance companies, banks, and other commercial mortgage-backed securities providers. My presentation was intended to show the audience members how to transition from CC 2 CC and create their own heartfelt All About Them positioning for their cerebral, numbers-based businesses.

I started by taking the audience through the subject of my last book, *Building Brand Value: Seven Simple Steps to Profitable Communications*. Then I explained the concept of moving from CC 2 CC and how to build an emotive connection with consumers that focused on the emotional benefits of working with their companies. Finally, I talked about the different ways the different people and companies in the audience could put these theories into practice.

Someone in the audience raised his hand. "What if we all follow your advice?" he asked. "Then we'll all wind up doing the same thing, and our marketing messages will all look alike. How's that going to help us?"

"Let's be honest," I countered. "If I were to come back here a year from now and stand up in front of this same group and ask you to raise your hands if you'd actually followed my advice and created a new, more emotional and customer-focused brand message that was powerfully All About Them, how many of you do you think would put your hands up?

"Truth is, few of you will actually implement this idea. Not because you don't think it'll work or don't want to do it, but because other things will get in the way. You'll get back to the office and clients' needs will take over. You'll mean to get your team together and work on this, but then you'll get busy and not find the time. To quote the Yiddish proverb: 'Men plan, God laughs.' Or maybe John Lennon put it best when he said, 'Life is what happens when you're busy making other plans.'

"But let's suppose you all actually do go through with it and create new All About Them brands. You still don't have to worry about your work being similar because you'll each bring something different to the process. You'll each build your brands around the authentic truths of your companies, and you'll use the power of your personal passions, and the results will be as different—and as diverse—as each one of you."

The notion that repeated techniques and themes create vastly different outcomes is neither new nor original. For example, Hunter College professor and Stanford Shakespeare scholar Gary Schmidgall, who has written extensively on both William Shakespeare and Oscar Wilde, points out that the supernatural picture, the main literary device of Wilde's *The Picture of Dorian Gray*, was not original to that author. Instead it was "astonishingly ubiquitous [appearing in] Gogol's *The Portrait*, Hawthorne's *Prophetic Picture* and Edward Randolph's *Portrait*, Disraeli's *Vivian Grey*, Henry James's *Story of a Masterpiece*, and Maturin's *Melmoth the Wanderer*." Plus, "dozens of other haunted pictures [can] be found in long-forgotten novels" written years before Wilde's masterpiece.

Wilde's book and so many others show us that while we all look at the human condition with the same eyes and often see the same things, we can still produce wildly different final products. It's not a matter of copying or plagiarizing what has come before; rather it's a matter of interpreting current events and activities in a way that is relevant for our readers, our clients, and our audiences.

After I finished my talk, I spent some time with Willy Walker, Walker & Dunlop's president. We discussed his company's services and how difficult it was to differentiate them from the competition without using the superlatives that companies in his industry used to describe themselves. We talked about different ways for Walker & Dunlop to build its CC 2 CC All About Them brand, and of course

I offered to help as Willy looked to incorporate these ideas into his company.

A few weeks later I got a note from Willy saying that he'd directed his marketing team to create the company's new positioning. He sent me examples of what the team had been working on, and we debated the various merits of what they were doing. We ended with an agreement that Willy would keep me up to date on their progress.

A few more weeks passed, and Willy again reached out and sent me the updated sketches of the proposed campaign. Once again we batted around different alternatives and talked about what would best achieve his goals. When we were done, Willy and his team went back to the drawing board to refine the concepts further.

The next time he contacted me, Willy sent not rough ideas but a finished campaign with this note:

Bruce: Happy New Year! I hope all is great with you.

I wanted to show you the work product that came from our discussions on an All About Them position for W&D.

As you can see, we changed the actual idea somewhat, but I think the overall campaign and messaging has been fantastic.

Our clients LOVE it, and we've been doing a new customer about every other month.

Please send news about things on your end.

All the best,

Willy

Attached to Willy's note was a PDF file with seven Walker & Dunlop ads. Each showed a picture of a W&D client participating in an activity he or she was passionate about. The ads also included the clients' names, a description of their passion, a time stamp showing how long they'd done business with W&D, and the line "Powering Your Prosperity."

Kurt Zech of Kennedy Wilson was shown surfing. Bob Hart of TruAmerica Multifamily was shown piloting his sailboat. Barry R. Mandel of the Mandel Group was shown swimming. David Schwartz of Waterton Residential was shown mountaineering. James Favrot of Favrot and Shane Companies was shown with his vintage car collection. Steve DeFrancis of Cortland Partners was shown walking hand in hand with his two children. And Michael Mouron of Capstone Companies was shown sitting alongside a uniformed wheelchair basketball player.

Each W&D client was described as an avid enthusiast. And the clear message was that because Walker & Dunlop had helped to power their prosperity, these individuals had the resources—time and money—to pursue their passions. Or as Willy put it in a subsequent e-mail, "They all capture distinct aspects of 'prosperity'—defined as anything you love doing that isn't work."

Notice that the passions were as different as the participants themselves. And W&D was placing no value judgment on their customers' passions. Instead the company was demonstrating its commitment to helping its clients accomplish whatever was important to them. And in so doing, W&D also fortified its relationship with each customer.

Interestingly, besides establishing W&D's brand positioning and demonstrating its All About Them mind-set, the ads themselves became both brag sheets and recruitment tools for the financial company's customers.

When Marshall McLuhan wrote that the medium is the message in 1967, he meant that how the message is distributed and presented is as important as the message itself. When he received the first edition of his book, he found that the printer had made a typo on the cover, changing McLuhan's now cliché phrase to "the medium is the *massage*." Legend has it that when he discovered the mistake, he said, "Leave it alone! It's great, and right on target!"

Were McLuhan around still, I believe he would agree that the medium of Walker & Dunlop's new campaign is both the message and the massage.

SO, WHAT DO YOU STAND FOR?

Walker & Dunlop has been in the real estate financing business for almost eighty years. It has at least twenty-five offices stretching from Arizona to Washington, DC. It works in all aspects of real estate financing. And it stands for facilitating its customers' prosperity.

Volvo is ostensibly in the car business. But that means it's really in a number of different businesses: transportation, manufacturing, research and development, metallurgy, engineering, upholstery, design, import/export, logistics, to name just a few. Plus, it operates retail stores (for both new and used products) and also provides sales, service, and accessories. Volvo operates under the governmental regulations of the hundreds of countries, states, and municipalities it operates in. It works in multiple languages, with multiple consumers, in multiple currencies. And don't forget that it doesn't just make consumer automobiles. Volvo also manufactures buses, trucks, and marine engines and provides engineering for lots of other companies. And yet, despite all of this incredible complexity, Volvo still describes itself through its commitment to one word: safety.

What do you stand for? Can you describe it in just a few words? If you can't, how can you expect your current and prospective clients to understand both who you are and why you matter to them? What difference will it make if you're tweeting your little heart out and Facebooking right and left if you're sending out random shotgun blasts instead of laser-focused marketing messages?

Believe it or not, I already know what you're thinking: Sure, Bruce, defining an issue and standing for something makes a lot of sense, and I can see how it works for all those companies. (Big sigh.) But I'm different. After all, my business is much more diverse, much more creative, and much more customized to my clients' specific needs . . . I do too many different things. There's just no way I could shoehorn everything I offer into a couple of words.

Really? Your business is too complicated to brand? Well, before we accept that and give up, let's look back at how Volvo defines itself.

Safety.

The safety brand positioning is so valuable to Volvo that when it introduced its SUV, arguably the new American suburban family car, the XC70 outsold all foreign SUVs (European and Asian) combined!

What's more, Volvo's brand description isn't even about the function its products actually provide. Nowhere does its branding talk about transportation or about getting from point A to point B. Volvo talks about safety.

New York is the Big Apple. Chicago is solidly Midwestern. Los Angeles is movies. Las Vegas is sin. Miami is hip. What are you?

FOX is on the right. MSNBC is on the left. CNN is firmly in the middle. Where are you?

The funny thing is, we use these designations every single day without thinking twice. Yet, when it comes to our own brand identity, the cobbler's kids have no shoes.

WHAT YOUR BRAND POSITION IS
AND WHAT IT'S NOT

So how do you figure out what your brand position is? Well, first let's talk about what it's not. Your brand position is not what you do; that's your vocation. Your brand is not what you believe in; those are your values. Your brand is not even what you do in your spare time (juggling, comedy, volunteering at the local hospital); that's your avocation.

Your brand position is not your business card, your tagline, or your talent. It's not your Facebook page, your Twitter handle, or your LinkedIn connections. And it's certainly not your logo.

Your brand position is the place you occupy in the heads and hearts of your current and potential customers. And if you don't know what that is, you can be sure they don't either.

That's the bad news.

The good news is that it's simple to figure out. With time and a lot of soul-searching, you can distill all of the great things you provide your customers down to a single, powerful, compelling essence. Please note that I said simple, not easy. Figuring out your brand positioning takes hard work. But if you follow one simple diagram and apply yourself to the process, you'll create a brand position that will help inform everything else you do and ensure that your future marketing efforts are efficient and effective.

SCALING THE PYRAMID TO SUCCESS

Ready to get started?

Take a look at the figure below. This is a classic brand pyramid. Hundreds, maybe even thousands, of great brands have been created using this simple triangle, and it will work just as well for you.

The way it works is simple: You just start filling in the boxes, going from the general (bottom) to the specific (top). When you reach the apex, you'll have a very good idea of what your brand position is and how to promote it to the world.

What You've Got

In the bottom box, "Features and Attributes," you inventory everything you and your business offer. And I mean everything. Here's where you list your products and services, your talents, skills, and

experience, and everything you use to run your business. Have a computer or two? Write it down. American Airlines frequent flier status? Down it goes. Suits and heels, brochures, and online products? Start scribbling. Specific industry experience, a unique life story, a killer résumé? They all belong in the box.

Needless to say, you don't have to actually write on the pyramid; you can create your files in Word or Excel or whatever program you like. How you record the information is unimportant. It matters that you do it clearly and well.

The more inclusive you make your list, the easier filling out the next level will be. Because the more complete your portfolio of attributes, the more you'll have to draw from as you scale the pyramid. It's no accident that this first section is at the bottom of the diagram. It serves as the foundation on which you'll build the rest of your brand messaging. The more comprehensive it is, the stronger your structure will be.

You also don't have to do this alone. If you have an assistant or other professionals in your business, they should participate as well. Your husband or wife or significant other can be a good source of information. Friends are good too, as are clients with whom you have a good personal relationship. You may even want to schedule an ideation session and have a bunch of people work together to list all of your company's features and attributes on big flip charts in your conference or living room. The bottom line is that you want to assemble as much pertinent data as possible. And don't worry about doing this all in one sitting. Often ideas will keep popping into your head long after you've turned off the computer and gone home. I don't care when you generate the list; I only care that you build it carefully and well.

What You Do Better Than Anyone Else and What Sets You Apart

Once you've completed the first section, it's time to move up a level to "POD," for "points of difference" or "points of distinction." Here you'll list your unique attributes. Perhaps you play harmonica (oh wait, that's what I do). That would go in this section. Maybe you have a proprietary coaching technique. That goes here too. Unusual physical or racial characteristics? If you use them to your advantage, write them down. Chances are that anything you consider your intellectual property, have trademarked or copyrighted, or use a special process or recipe for belongs in this list as well.

I'm sure you know that the word "unique" is absolute: you're either unique or you're not; you can't be a little unique anymore than you can be a little perfect, a little excellent, or a little pregnant. Please don't take the word "unique" literally. If it's true that there's nothing new under the sun, then there's a pretty good chance that whatever your unique attributes, you're not the only person in the entire universe who will list them. Still, items listed here, alone or perhaps in combination, should give you a unique slant or delivery. If an attribute is not special and doesn't set you apart, then it belongs in the first category, not the second.

For example, Volvo isn't the only car company that spends time and money on safety. It's even arguable whether or not a Volvo is safer than similar models produced by the competition. But Volvo has invested so much effort into building its brand around safety that this has become one of its most valuable and differentiating attributes. Therefore, other car companies would probably include safety in their attributes slot but wouldn't include it in the POD section. Volvo would.

When you're done, this list should be a lot shorter than that for "Features and Attributes." It should contain only the items that are uniquely yours: specific deliverables that you own and that your clients and audiences will readily identify with you and you alone. You don't need to worry if you don't have a lot of items on this list—many fortunes have been built on just one powerful POD. But if you can't add anything compelling or anything truly unique and special to the list, then your problem is more fundamental than branding. If you've got nothing that's uniquely your own, you'd better get to work on your product before you even think about marketing. After all, Paul Revere probably would not have gone down in history if he'd ridden through the colonial night warning the populace, "The British may or may not be coming."

What You Do

Now it's time to ratchet up to the next level: "Functional Benefits." To fill out this section you've got to put on a different hat and start thinking like your customer. You want to list the functional benefits your consumer will get from doing business with you. So if you consult on safety preparedness, your clients will know how to outfit and organize their business for a disaster. If you study family businesses and create succession strategies, then after working with you, your clients will understand how to plan for the successful transition between generations.

And if you write about social media, then your readers will understand how to incorporate Twitter, Facebook, LinkedIn, and so forth, into their businesses.

This section is the easiest because it's the most obvious. And it's where most businesses stop when they think about their brands—if they think about them in the first place. They start with what they've got (features and attributes), ladder up to what they're good at and known for (POD), and then focus on what they do for their customers (functional benefits).

So if I owned a little café in an industrial park, for instance, I would first list my features and attributes and come up with a list that included our tables and chairs, our signage, our kitchen equipment, and so on. For POD, I'd list our better recipes and our delivery. If my café were the only restaurant in the industrial compound, I'd probably include our exclusive location as well.

Next, I'd ladder up the chart and look at the functional benefits we supplied to our customers. Obviously the most functional benefit of all would be filling their bellies, but I'd like to think we'd be a little more sophisticated than that. So I might add things such as our location's allowing our clients to eat lunch without having to go very far and our ability to cater office meetings and presentations. Maybe I'd include the opportunity for our customers to drive to work an hour early to avoid traffic and have breakfast with us. Perhaps I'd include that we offered prepared foods in the evening so that working couples who didn't have time to prepare a delicious, nutritious meal could pick up a completely prepared dinner for their families before heading home.

The magic starts to happen at the next level of the pyramid: "Emotional Benefits." Because here you really begin to connect with your audiences. And you can only get there if you've already been very clear about your functional benefits.

How They Feel

Remember that Volvo's brand doesn't really talk about its cars' functional benefits. Instead, Volvo has built a powerful brand based on the emotional benefits of safety. Thanks to Volvo's product attributes and brand messaging, Volvo drivers can feel that they're better parents, better spouses, and better citizens because they're driving a safer car. And because this benefit lives in the heart and not the head, it stands to reason that it's a less intellectual but much more powerful approach. Words that fit in this messaging category include "confidence," "reassurance," "fulfillment," "relief," and "love"—all of which help Volvo build a strong emotional bond with its current and potential customers.

Top o' the World, Ma

Once you've filled in the emotional benefits, look back at the pyramid and look for the connection between what you offer (POD) and what your customer will feel when you've done your job (emotional benefits). These patterns will become the fuel for the creative inspiration that you'll need in order to fill in the final triangle at the very top of the pyramid—which is where great brand definitions live. Here you'll find taglines like "Just do it,"

"There is no substitute," "The relentless pursuit of perfection," "I love New York," and "We'll leave the light on for you."

These lines, none more than seven words long, exemplify how great brands connect viscerally and emotionally with consumers. You'll notice that none of them talks about what the product actually does. Instead, each evokes the feelings that users will enjoy when they engage with the brand itself. And this is the All About Them place where you want your brand to live.

You Did It! Welcome to All About Them

Filling in the final section of the pyramid is the hardest part of constructing your brand positioning. Because besides the craftsmanship and eloquence required, moving from CC 2 CC and figuring out a truly unique consumer-focused and emotional brand message takes a lot of work and trial and error. But once you climb to the top of the pyramid and proclaim who you are and what you stand for, the rest of your marketing is easy. With your brand positioning firmly established, you'll know what your ads should look like, how your website should function, and what you should tweet. Knowing your powerful brand position will also help you pick subjects to take a stand on and topics to write about. And, most importantly, when you begin to promote and distribute your brand messaging, it will tell your current and potential customers what to expect from you and which leads to refer to you. Because once you, your employees, and your current and potential customers know what you stand for, the rest of the business becomes that much easier.

WHAT HAVE YOU LEARNED?

To incorporate a successful All About Them strategy, it's important to understand the difference between products and services you create for yourself and those you create for your customers. Because of this, it's important to understand how your customers' needs, tastes, and budgets may differ from your own. There are selling ties and wearing ties, after all.

At the same time, if we only concentrate our production on what our clients and customers want, we will simply create more and more generic products that have no differentiation and cannot effectively compete in a rapidly expanding marketplace. This is why it's also critical to understand your authentic truth and incorporate it into your brand messaging. Always remember that a good brand makes people feel good, but a great brand makes people feel good about themselves. Walker & Dunlop's new ad campaign took the company's essence and distilled it into a message that not only showed how the financial services company drove its clients' success but also celebrated its customers' passions and accomplishments.

Knowing what you stand for is a great way to begin to build this sense of authenticity in order to transfer your brand identity to the people you do business with. If the saying used to be "You are what you eat," today it's evolved into "You are what you consume." In today's consumer age, people count on the products they buy and the services they use to tell the world who they are. While our parents' generations were known for the wars they fought, today's generations are known for the things they buy. Standing for something allows your customer to enjoy the added value of buying your product or service and your badge.

Knowing who you are and communicating this positioning not only helps your customers know what they're getting when they purchase your products or agree with your viewpoints; it also helps them sell you to others. And when your customers build their own brand identifications around the one you provide, their endorsement becomes a further referral source that will drive other customers to you and your business.

In Chapter 6 we explored how Bill O'Reilly has built a congruent brand around the authentic truth of who he is and what his customers want to watch. But I didn't tell you what happened after I appeared on O'Reilly's program.

Sometime in the middle of my interview, O'Reilly pointed at me and said, "You're wrong again, Mr. Turkel. You're zero for two." And then, near the end of the interview, he added a sarcastic, "Well, Mr. Turkel, you were O for two, but now you've just brought up a brilliant point."

At the time of my appearance, O'Reilly's program regularly attracted one of the largest audiences in the news business—nearly 3 million viewers. Of course I was pleased about gaining exposure to an audience of that size, but the best result was when I sent a video clip of my time in O'Reilly's hot seat to my clients and potential clients. Not only did I enjoy the borrowed prestige of having been on *The O'Reilly Factor*, but my clients too could enhance their brand value by telling their shareholders that they worked with the guy who had appeared on O'Reilly's show.

The funny thing is, the clip I sent did not include O'Reilly telling me how smart I was or agreeing with me. On the contrary, he repeatedly pointed out that I was wrong. But O'Reilly's objections were as irrelevant as whether or not any of my points were actually correct. The benefit of being on his show derived not from being right but from being on his show in the first place. O'Reilly expressed his authentic truth, I expressed mine, and we both benefitted from the exchange.

In the end, the best marketing opportunities tend to be quid pro quo exchanges like that one. Both participants bring their value to the table (knowledge, audience, talent, appearance, fame, point of view, eloquence, whatever) and benefit from the chance to both expose their attributes and enhance the other participant's brand value. And when you know what your true All About Them brand is and how to communicate it, you can extract the full value of these opportunistic exchanges. After all, as the Roman philosopher Seneca reminded us, "Luck is what happens when preparation meets opportunity."

So now that you know how to create your All About Them brand, there are just two things left to do: walk the walk, and talk the talk.

9

WALKING YOUR WALK, TALKING YOUR TALK

PRACTICE MAKES PERFECT

Practice makes perfect, but nobody's perfect. Why practice?

THE IRONY OF PRACTICE

There are people who make a practice of not positioning themselves across from me at board meetings. That's because I spend my time in those meetings drawing caricatures of everyone sitting around the conference table. Actually, I draw pictures of everyone except the people seated directly alongside me. That's because I can't really draw my neighbors without constantly turning my head and not paying attention to what's going on in the meeting itself.

Believe it or not, a number of people don't like having me draw them. I think it's probably because I don't draw portraits;

I draw caricatures. As I understand it, good portraits are usually realistic representations of the people showcased, whereas good caricatures generally exaggerate and lampoon a subject's most prominent features. That's why royalty and aristocrats throughout history commissioned famous artists to paint the regal portraits that now hang in museums around the world and caricatures were relegated to carnival midways and biting editorial cartoons. It's also why people who actually look at the drawings I've done of them tend to say, "That's funny. But my nose isn't that big, is it?" Or "Oh, c'mon. I really have more hair than that, don't I?"

Those are the comments of the people I've drawn. But the people who sit next to me and see what I'm doing during the meeting usually say something like, "I wish I could draw. But I'm not talented like that. You're a natural."

My answer is always the same: "Of course you can draw. All you have to do is draw . . . a lot."

"Oh, you mean like practice?" they ask. "How much do you practice?"

"I don't ever practice," I answer. "But I do draw all the time. Come to think of it, I've been doing it since kindergarten. I was on the newspaper staff in high school, and I studied art and design in college. And when I started working in advertising, I started as a studio artist and then became an art director. I've been drawing every day of my life for as long as I can remember."

In his book *Outliers*, Malcolm Gladwell suggests that it requires roughly 10,000 hours of practice to achieve mastery. A great example Gladwell uses to make his point is the rise of The Beatles. In the early 1960s, the nascent "Fab Four" played their hearts out in the basements of the Kaiserkeller and Indra clubs and other small venues throughout Hamburg, Germany. The band was so driven that it had played nearly 1,200 public performances before returning to England and becoming the most influential rock band in history. Those 1,200 gigs provided The Beatles with the 10,000 hours of practice Gladwell says mastery requires. In other words, The Beatles were an "overnight success" after years of hard work.

But more matters than just the hours invested. How the practice is performed is also important. As I see it, the key to developing and utilizing talent is not just to put in the hours but to make the participation a natural part of your life.

Sure, a musician has to practice the rudiments and learn the scales in every conceivable mode and key. Of course an artist needs to understand the opportunities and limits of various media and techniques. And yes, an athlete and a dancer must practice their fundamentals time and time again until muscle memory takes over. But there's more to it than that.

Everyone's heard Confucius's expression "Choose a job you love, and you will never have to work a day in your life." I've discovered that this adage applies to talent too. The real key to learning to draw or to mastering tennis or the clarinet or to earning your black belt in judo—or whatever—is to love doing it so much that you do it because you want to, not because you have to.

Taken further, the key to mastery is to develop the various talents that are an intrinsic component of who you are so that not only isn't practice something that you have to do or even that you want to do; it's something you do without planning or even thinking about it beforehand. You do it because it's a part of who you are. The saying in Spanish is *Eso le nace*, meaning literally, "It's born in you."

Seen from a business angle, rehearsing your skill sets also becomes a crucial part of developing and building your brand value. That's because what you're about sets you and your company apart from the competition and lets your customers know what's in it for them. As I've said so many times before, people don't choose what you do; they choose who you are.

Knowing this—and knowing how to present it to your customers and potential customers—is the way to not only incorporate your intrinsic talents into your personal and professional lives but to get better and better at what you do and to enjoy it even more than you do already.

BUILDING CONSENSUS AROUND YOUR BRAND

So let's say that you've now figured out what your brand is all about. You've figured out your messaging and how to make it All About Them, how to make it emotional, how to make it simple, how to make it quick. You now know how to make your brand positioning ownable and sensual. In short, you know who you are and how and why you matter to your current and potential customers.

Remember the old nursery rhyme about the bear that went over the mountain? If you do then, please sing along (preferably in your best Huckleberry Hound howling *Oh Susanna!* voice):

> *The bear went over the mountain,*
> *The bear went over the mountain,*
> *The bear went over the mountain,*

And what do you think he saw?
He saw another mountain,
He saw another mountain,
He saw another mountain,
That's what the bear saw.

Well congratulations. Because now that you've gotten over the mountain and done the serious work of identifying your brand, you'll find that now you're looking up at the next mountain you have to climb. In other words, it's time to get your message out to your public.

Lots of great books have been written on how to market your brand—from Howard Gossage's classic essays collected in *The Book of Gossage* to David Ogilvy's *Confessions of an Advertising Man* to Michael Bierut's *How to Use Graphic Design to Sell Things, Explain Things, Make Things Look Better, Make People Laugh, Make People Cry, and Every Once in a While Change the World*. If you've gotten this far and you're turned on by the idea of creatively marketing your brand, I suggest you read them all.

In the meantime, what are you going to do to build consensus behind your brand? After all, you didn't do all this work just to create a great message that nobody hears, did you?

It's time to walk your talk.

You see, it's not enough to know what you stand for and how your brand resonates with your various audiences. It's time to push your little brand birdie out of the nest and let it fly. To completely mix my metaphors, it don't mean a thing (if it ain't got that swing). It matters now that you aggressively communicate your brand value in a cogent, coherent, consistent manner.

THE THREE Cs

Three alliterative nouns—cogency, coherency, and consistency—
are the essential horsemen of your new brand communication
and are critical to its ongoing success. Let's look at them in-
dividually and explore how you can use them to build your
brand value.

Cogency

Most of the advertising and marketing messages you see today
are crap. They're watered-down, meaningless bundles of pablum created mostly to keep everyone involved from getting
into trouble. Unfortunately, as my pal Randy Gage points out
in his two most recent books, *Risky Is the New Safe* and *Mad
Genius*, that kind of safe, CYA attitude is the most expensive
mistake you can make. Because while you're busy trying not
to offend or upset anyone, you're also not getting anyone's
attention or changing anyone's mind.

By making sure that your All About Them brand communications have a cogent connection to your brand, you'll also con-
firm that they are doing the job you want them to do. That is,
they are promoting your specific message and making sure that
it resonates with your consumers, intelligently informing and
reminding them why they should be doing business with you.

Coherency

So much of what you see online and on the airwaves today
is such garbage because the marketers creating the messaging

forget whom they are actually creating the messages for. In this instance the evil is doubled because different people in the ad agencies, marketing firms, and in-house advertising departments are serving different masters and marching to very different drummers. If you are working in or with one of these companies, the following is an important paradigm for you to be both aware and wary of.

On the one hand, marketing companies (both in-house and outsourced) are staffed with people charged with servicing and maintaining their accounts. While it would appear that their primary motivation would be to help their clients build their businesses, the real-life observation is that their main function is not to piss anyone off and not to lose their clients' business. These are the people parodied in every TV show and movie that features advertising, from *Bewitched* to *Nothing in Common* to *Mad Men* to *Shark Tank*. While their titles range from account executive to client manager, their overwhelming desire is to cover their asses and not rock the boat. Perhaps the old lightbulb jokes say it best:

Q: "How many junior account executives does it take to change a lightbulb?"

A: "I don't know sir, but I'll find out and get right back to you."

Q: "How many senior account executives does it take to change a lightbulb?"

A: "How many would you like?"

Clearly these people are more concerned with how they look than how you can cogently express your brand value, and you generally can't count on them to provide good, smart answers to your most pressing questions.

But before you think I'm a typical ad agency "creative" who looks down his nose at account executives and regards them as little more than delivery boys and girls, let me share two different opinions.

First, good account executives—the ones who really understand strategy and are willing to stick their necks out specifically to help their clients make the right decisions and run the right messages—are as valuable as they are rare. These very special people can make all the difference in the world and truly help their clients build their brand value and reach their goals.

Second, I think that the group even more responsible for all of the bad branding messages we're exposed to includes not toadying account executives but misguided and overzealous art directors, writers, and designers.

These people are so intent on "being creative" that they often forget why they're creating branding messages in the first place. Whether it's a desire to win awards (after movies and music, advertising and marketing are the most self-congratulatory industries on earth), to build a portfolio financed by their clients' marketing budgets, or simply to emulate the great work that's come before, these people create messages based on their ability to titillate, shock, and win prizes, not to persuade and influence consumers.

Of course they have their own lightbulb jokes:

Q: "How many copywriters does it take to change a lightbulb?"

A: "None. That's my work, and I'm not changing a goddamned thing."

Q: "How many art directors does it take to change a lightbulb?"

A: "Does it have to be a lightbulb? I was reading *Communication Arts Magazine*, and I think there are some choices that are more *now*."

Q: "How many creative directors does it take to change a lightbulb?"

A: "Two. One to hold the lightbulb and one to keep drinking until the house starts spinning."

A coherent message is created solely and specifically to enhance the brand value it is intended to support. There is no other competing motivation other than coherently enriching your agreed-upon brand value.

Consistency

Marketing people love to put skillsets and messages into various silos. Hang around enough of them, and you'll hear the phrases "above the line" and "below the line." You'll hear about "online" messages and "traditional" messages. You'll hear about "advertising," "marketing," "promotions," and "public relations." You'll confront "paid media" and "earned media." You'll also hear about "on- and off-premises." In fact, you'll probably hear as many categories as there are marketing people.

The problem is that not only don't consumers know about these different terms; they don't care about them either. So when potential buyers see a brand message on a billboard, then read an article about it, then see a pop-up ad on a favorite website, they don't say that they have "interacted with the brand in out-of-home media; an earned, PR placement; and an online banner ad"; they say simply, "I see it everywhere."

But it's not just a matter of message distribution and media. A commitment to consistency means that every message presented and received should reference and reinforce every other message.

THE IRONY OF CONSISTENCY

As we've already seen, a number of very complex branded products sell themselves with cogent, coherent, and consistent messages.

Volvo has been selling safety since the 1970s. And insurance companies Allstate and Prudential have been presenting themselves using "You're in good hands with Allstate" and "Get a piece of the rock" for even longer.

Knowing who you are and what you stand for is not just a great way to build your All About Them brand; it's ultimately a real money saver because it both focuses your outreach efforts and makes sure that each message you promote reinforces every other one you've already delivered and the new messages yet to come.

Ironically, an All About Them brand's need for consistency does not give you the right to be repetitive. If you simply repeat the same old message over and over, your audience will eventually become immune to the power of your communication and simply ignore it or even become turned off by it.

Instead, you must commit to coming up with new, exciting ways to say the same old thing. (By the way, that means job security for the best of the copywriters, designers, and art directors we talked about a few paragraphs ago.)

In an effort to enforce consistency in its brand message, BMW has been "The ultimate driving machine" since 1972. But over the succeeding decades its cars have changed drastically—from early-1970s 2002s and Bavarias to today's 1, 2, 3, 4, 5, 6, 7, 8, I, M, X, and Z series. What's more, where BMW once sold cars powered by gasoline or diesel fuel, today you can buy BMWs that not only run on those two energy sources but are also energized by batteries, hybrid power, plug-ins, and hydrogen fuel cells.

To coordinate its offerings and maintain its brand consistency in light of such a wide product offering, BMW now runs an ad that lists all the different products it sells. The ad features beauty shots of the company's convertibles, SUVs, luxury cars, hybrids, and electric vehicles—highlighting the fact that they're all as different from each other as can be—and then ties them all together by announcing, "At BMW we only make one thing . . . The ultimate driving machine."

#ISM

My advertising agency has been responsible for marketing the Miami tourism brand for the last twenty-five years or so. Our work for William Talbert and the Greater Miami Convention and Visitors Bureau has always been about ways to craft a compelling All About Them brand. Using our seven points of building brand value, we've been cogent, coherent, and consistent, always selling Miami's authentic truth as a one-of-a-kind tropical and cosmopolitan experience, while being careful to stay relevant to a changing tourist audience.

After all, we needed to sell Miami when *Time* magazine's cover story called our community "Paradise Lost." We needed to sell Miami after the horrors of 9/11 virtually shut down air travel across the country (when 98 percent of Miami's visitors arrive via airplane). We needed to sell Miami when northern winters experienced record warm temperatures, and we needed to sell Miami when our chief audience appeal shifted from beaches and warm weather to arts and culture. Bottom line? We needed to fill our beaches and hotels regardless of how our neighborhoods—and the world around us—continued to change.

To really recognize how complicated our challenge is, you also need to look into the realities of our community a little deeper. After all, while many people hear "Miami" and think of an airport and the glitz of South Beach, the city is home to a very sophisticated and complicated community with a diverse population and topography.

Even if you live here, you probably don't know that Miami–Dade County consists of thirty-six different municipalities, most with their own city government and services. The county is home to three national parks; the largest collection of art deco architecture in the world; an ocean, a bay, a river, and myriad lakes; and prairie land, hardwood hammocks, independent islands, pinewood forests, and swampland. And of course we're bordered by the Everglades in the west and the Atlantic Ocean in the east.

You probably also didn't know that Miami–Dade County is an education powerhouse. With almost 350,000 students from more than one hundred countries, its public school system is the largest in Florida and the fourth largest in the country. The county benefits from more than twenty colleges and universities, including Miami Dade College, the largest and most robust college on the planet, with eight campuses and more than 170,000 students from around the world; Florida International University, which is one of the country's twenty-five largest universities; Barry University, a Catholic institution that is over seventy years old; and, of course, the University of Miami. The county also houses the busiest cruise port in the world, and its airport has the largest cargo volume in the country and served almost 27 million passengers in 2015.

I list all of this not to brag about my hometown but to show you just a little bit of how complicated, multifaceted, and heterogeneous it is.

Of course that means our tourism product is just as multi-dimensional and complicated. Visitors to what they describe as "Miami" can stay in South Beach, Miami Beach, Surfside, Sunny Isles, Bal Harbour, Aventura, North Miami Beach, Coral Gables, Coconut Grove, Brickell, Doral, and more. And while they're there, they can visit all those towns as well as Homestead, Little Havana, Little Haiti, South Miami, Little Managua (officially called Sweetwater), Wynwood, the Design District, Morningside, Golden Beach, Eastern Shores, and many more communities.

Still, all of these choices are branded under one name with only five letters: *M-I-A-M-I.* And the experiences that all of these areas contribute are explained with three words—"It's so Miami"—along with a three-letter hashtag: #ISM.

It's So Miami tells consumers that they'll see things in Miami that they simply won't see anywhere else. They'll experience things they can't experience anywhere else. And at the end of the day, they'll be able to do the things they want to do and be the people they want to be with a freedom and abandon that they simply cannot enjoy anywhere else in the world.

Because of the languages we speak, the countries we come from, the freewheeling way we were formed, the liberal mores we embrace, and even the balmy weather we enjoy, It's So Miami means you can be who you are and who you want to be.

A quick review of our advertising and marketing messages will show how this attitude has informed our communication and empowered us to build our tourism business by always staying true to our authentic selves and being cogent, coherent, and consistent.

Our ads show people having Miami experiences you simply could not have in another city—from wearing a bikini in an art museum (unheard of elsewhere, commonplace in Miami), to dressing like an international fashion model on our beaches, to parking your $300,000 orange sports car long enough to order a twenty-five-cent *cafecito*. But how that message gets communicated in all of our outreach efforts confirms our commitment to being cogent, coherent, and consistent.

Because of Miami's importance as a regional shipping powerhouse, our cargo port is installing new gantry cranes—the giant, 260-foot-tall behemoths that load and unload goods shipped from Asia and Latin America to the rest of the country and throughout the region. These giant structures puncture the skylines of lots of cargo ports from Savannah to Singapore. But only in Miami could we recommend to the mayor and the County Commission that they paint the cranes pink and black, effectively creating a flock of 260-foot-tall flamingos.

More importantly, only in Miami could we make that suggestion without being laughed out of the room. Why? Because It's So Miami!

But here's the best part: Say the County Commission approves our idea and the cranes get painted (at the time *All About Them* went to press, we hadn't yet gotten approval). And let's further suggest that we get all of the worldwide coverage that we expect. What happens if other competing communities try to copy our idea? What if Savannah were to paint its cranes to look like giant storks and Tampa painted its cranes to look like great herons? At best they would only create flamingo-like cranes that referenced the original Miami cranes. After all, both the skinny pink birds and the idea of painting giant structures bright pink are consistent with Miami's authentic truth.

And what will people say when they see the giant pink cranes in any other community? It's So Miami!

IT'S ONLY A RISK IF IT DOESN'T FIT— OR IF YOU DON'T DO IT

I hope it's clear by now that once you've done the work necessary to uncover your All About Them brand, the resulting construct will provide you with both the license and the courage to promote it. After all, if the brand you've created both adheres to your authentic truth and resonates with your potential customers, then the only risk you'll take is not promoting it in every cogent, coherent, and consistent way you can think of.

What's more, owning and promoting your very own All About Them positioning will give you access to opportunities you never thought possible and may never have come up with on your own. That's because if your brand properly resonates with your intended public, it will fire people's imaginations and give them tacit permission to figure out ways to work with you and promote your brand and your business because it's good for them too.

Not a week goes by that I don't field invitations to speak at corporate events or bring my band to community festivals or help a company or an individual build a unique brand. That's because my All About Them strategy opens people's eyes to what they can do and encourages them to look for ways for us to work together.

If I'm completely honest, I have to admit that their interest, flattering as it might be on the surface, is not actually about me. Instead, the people who are calling and sending e-mails with invitations and opportunities are able to visualize ways that they can reach their goals by working with me. After hearing what I've said on TV or reading one of my books or blog posts or seeing me speak at an event they attended, they were able to imagine how doing business with me could better their lives.

AND IN THE END . . .

Thanks to my All About Them brand, people I don't know have been able to imagine how their lives could be better by joining with me.

That truly defines the power of All About Them. It's how I've built my business, encouraged my friendships, developed my deep and satisfying relationships, and continued to grow and evolve.

President Lyndon Johnson's secretary of health, education, and welfare, John W. Gardner, spelled it out quite clearly: "Life is an endless unfolding, and if we wish it to be, an endless process of self-discovery, an endless and unpredictable dialogue between our own potentialities and the life situations in which we find ourselves."

I wish most for you that you will look deep into yourself, find your authentic truth hidden in plain sight, communicate it in a way that speaks to your intended audiences, and reap all the benefits that you so richly deserve.

Nothing would make me happier than knowing that this book served as both the motivation and the tool to help you reach your greatest potential. Because that will transition my concept from All About Them to all about you.

All you have to do is do it. To quote Gardner again, "The only stability possible is stability in motion."

Thank you. Brand on. And please let me know how All About Them works for you. I'm quite eager to hear about your great success.

#AllAboutThem.

NOTES

INTRODUCTION

7   In 2003 Toyota released its second-generation hybrid: "Toyota Prius," Wikipedia, https://en.wikipedia.org/wiki/Toyota_Prius.

9   The proof is in the sales numbers: "Honda Civic Hybrid," Wikipedia, https://en.wikipedia.org/wiki/Honda_Civic_Hybrid.

9   In July 2007 the *New York Times* quoted a CNW Marketing Research finding: "Say 'Hybrid' and Many People Will Hear 'Prius,'" *New York Times*, July 4, 2007, http://www.nytimes.com/2007/07/04/business/04hybrid.html?_r=0.

9   *Washington Post* columnist Robert Samuelson coined the term "Prius politics": "It's All About Efficiency," *Washington Post*, August 4, 2007, http://www.washingtonpost.com/wp-dyn/content/article/2007/08/03/AR2007080301812.html.

9   Former Central Intelligence Agency (CIA) chief R. James Woolsey Jr. even went so far as to say: R. James Woolsey,

"How Your Gas Money Funds Terrorism" (presentation to the American Jewish Committee, Washington, DC, October 19, 2009), https://www.youtube.com/watch?v=jNDiQUBjR1o.

10 **"I have a bumper sticker on the back of my Prius":** Ben Oliver, "Oil Warrior," *Motor Trend Magazine*, May 2, 2007, http://www.motortrend.com/news/james-woolsey-interview.

10 **"Hollywood's latest politically correct status symbol":** "Prius Still Excites," *Independent*, March 25, 2012, http://independent.co.ug/society/motoring-/5451-prius-still-excites #sthash.LjvRomnc.dpuf.

17 **Obama raised $760,370,195, more than twice as much as McCain's $358,008,447:** "Fundraising for the 2008 United States Presidential Election," Wikipedia, https://en.wikipedia.org/wiki/Fundraising_for_the_2008_United _States_presidential_election.

21 **"Pulling the plug on grandma":** Brian Montopoli, "Grassley Warns of Government Pulling Plug 'on Grandma,'" CBS News, August 12, 2009, http://www.cbsnews.com/news/grassley -warns-of-government-pulling-plug-on-grandma.

CHAPTER 1

30 **"These arrangements were made on the website Task-Rabbit":** Mark Milian, "Apple IPhone 5 Store Lines Include Hundreds Getting Paid to Wait," *Bloomberg Business*, September 21, 2012, http://www.bloomberg.com/news/articles /2012-09-21/apple-iphone-5-store-lines-include-hundreds- getting-paid-to-wait.

31 **The term "First World problems" first appeared in a 1979 article by G. K. Payne in *Built Environment*:** G. K. Payne, "Housing: Third World Solutions to First World Problems," *Built Environment* 5, no. 2 (January 1, 1979): 99, http://search .proquest.com/openview/35913e79a5b6f935687af70613 b399e3/1?pq-origsite=gscholar&cbl=1817159.

35   "Ew, I start this f*** a** job tomorrow": cellla., Twitter, February 7, 2015, https://twitter.com/cellla__/status/564099253182554112.

36   One article, headlined "With an Apology, Brian Williams Digs Himself Deeper in Copter Tale": Jonathan Mahler, Ravi Somaiya, and Emily Steel, "With an Apology, Brian Williams Digs Himself Deeper in Copter Tale," *New York Times*, February 5, 2015, http://www.nytimes.com/2015/02/06/business/brian-williamss-apology-over-iraq-account-is-challenged.html.

36   The other, headlined "Pascal Lands in Sony's Outbox": Michael Cieply and Brooks Barnes, "Amy Pascal Lands in Sony's Outbox," New York Times, February 5, 2015, http://www.nytimes.com/2015/02/06/business/amy-pascal-leaving-as-sony-studio-chief.html.

37   The NBC host had a five-year, $10 million contract with the network: Brian Stelter, "NBC Trying to Keep Brian Williams—but Maybe Not as 'Nightly News' Anchor," *CNN Money*, May 31, 2015, http://money.cnn.com/2015/05/31/media/brian-williams-nbc-future.

37   Sony's executive's exit included a four-year guaranteed payout of $30 to $40 million: Cieply and Barnes, "Amy Pascal Lands in Sony's Outbox."

41   In 2014 Victoria's Secret UK showed a lineup of beautiful young: "That Campaign Against the Victoria's Secret 'Perfect Body' Ad?," *Independent*, http://indy100.independent.co.uk/article/that-campaign-against-the-victorias-secret-perfect-body-ad-it-worked--eks3-sVHwe.

44   "The two years of data collection shows": Chris Shunk, "TomTom Data Reveals US Drivers' Average Speed, Fastest Highway," *AutoBlog*, January 26, 2010, http://www.autoblog.com/2010/01/26/tomtom-data-reveals-u-s-drivers-average-speed-fastest-highway.

CHAPTER 2

53   "The computer is like electronic cocaine": Tony Dok-
      oupil, "Is The Internet Making Us Crazy? What the New Re-
      search Says," *Newsweek*, July 9, 2012, http://www.newsweek
      .com/internet-making-us-crazy-what-new-research-says
      -65593.

53   "The average person, regardless of age, sends or receives
      about 400 texts a month": Dokoupil, "Is The Internet
      Making Us Crazy?"

56   "The average user now picks up their device more than
      1,500 times a week": Victoria Woollaston, "How Often Do
      YOU Look at Your Phone?," *Daily Mail*, October 14, 2014,
      http://www.dailymail.co.uk/sciencetech/article-2783677
      /How-YOU-look-phone-The-average-user-picks-device
      -1-500-times-day.html#ixzz41mli5e75.

57   "The research firm Forrester estimates that e-commerce is
      now approaching $200 billion in revenue": Darrell Rigby,
      "The Future of Shopping," *Harvard Business Review*, December
      2011, https://hbr.org/2011/12/the-future-of-shopping.

61   "unprecedented access to what may become the largest on-
      line body of human knowledge": "Google Books," Wikipedia,
      https://en.m.wikipedia.org/wiki/Google_Books#Timeline.

61   "the democratization of knowledge": "Democratization
      of Knowledge," Project Gutenberg Self-Publishing Press,
      http://gutenberg.us/articles/democratization_of_knowledge.

62   "It used to take 10 or 12 minutes to get a clip into an Avid
      editor": Tony Maglio, "The Secret Weapon Behind 'Daily
      Show,' 'Colbert Report' and 'The Soup,'" *Wrap*, June 11, 2014,
      http://www.thewrap.com/the-secret-to-daily-show-colbert
      -report-and-the-soup-snapstream.

64   "Doing what's best for patients won't necessarily make
      them happy": Kevin Pho, "Be Wary of Doctor-Rating Sites,"

USA Today, September 14, 2014, http://www.usatoday .com/story/opinion/2014/09/14/kevin-pho-doctor-ratings -medicine-health-patient-satisfaction-column/15340309.

CHAPTER 3

68 **"The valuation of a bit is determined, in large part by its ability to be used over and over again"**: Nicholas Negroponte, *Being Digital* (New York: Alfred A. Knopf, 1995).

72 **"How Ya Gonna Keep 'Em Down on the Farm (After They've Seen Paree?)"**: "How Ya Gonna Keep 'Em Down on the Farm (After They've Seen Paree?), Music: Walter Donaldson, lyrics: Joe Young and Sam M. Lewis. Published: 1919, Waterson, Berlin & Snyder Co in New York.

77 **Louis C.K. was going on about the most innovative technology of the day**: "Everything's Amazing, Nobody's Happy," YouTube, February 29, 2009, https://www.youtube .com/watch?v=q8LaT5Iiwo4.

90 **But the videos of people dumping ice water on their heads**: Mark Holan, "Ice Bucket Challenge Has Raised $220 Million Worldwide," *Washington Business Journal*, December 12, 2014, http://www.bizjournals.com/washington/news/2014/12/12 /ice-bucket-challenge-has-raised-220-million.html.

92 **Rolls-Royce's painstakingly installing 1,340 fiber-optic 92 in the $12,000 starlight leather headliners of their Wraith two-door coupe**: "Under the Stars," Rolls Royce Motorcars, https://www.rolls-roycemotorcars.com/en-GB /bespoke/under-the-stars.html.

99 **Jeff Meshel, author of *The Opportunity Magnet*, started the original group in New York City**: Jeff Meshel, *The Opportunity Magnet* (Hobart, NY: Hatherleigh Press, 2010).

102 **Campbell's theory of the "monomyth" held that all great myths and stories throughout history are simply variations**

of one metamyth: Joseph Campbell, *The Hero with a Thousand Faces* (New York: Pantheon Books, 1949).

111   "Our customers are shopping not so much because of a desire to buy": Geoff Weiss, "How a 10-Minute Spot on QVC Turned This Woman into a $100 Million Cosmetics Mogul," *Entrepreneur Magazine*, http://www.entrepreneur.com/article/237379.

CHAPTER 4

125   "there are no naming metrics, no real way to know if a new name helps or hinders": Neal Gabler, "The Weird Science of Naming New Products," *New York Times Magazine*, January 15, 2015, http://www.nytimes.com/2015/01/18/magazine/the-weird-science-of-naming-new-products.html.

128   "For years, Starbucks marketed itself as a 'third place,' an 'affordable luxury'": Panos Mourdoukoutas, "Starbucks: From a Third Place to Another First Place," *Forbes*, October 26, 2014, http://www.forbes.com/sites/panosmourdoukoutas/2014/10/26/starbucks-from-a-third-place-to-another-first-place/#cb651d06f8c3.

CHAPTER 5

141   Daniel Pink explained that the way to assure business success is to create a compelling product persona that no one can copy: Daniel Pink, *A Whole New Mind* (New York: Riverhead Books, 2005).

CHAPTER 6

164   Tom Brokaw wrote the book about the generation of Americans who grew up during the Great Depression and fought in World War II: Tom Brokaw, *The Greatest Generation* (New York: Random House, 2004).

169 One study, financed in part by Samsung, investigated how consumers' identification with a brand's attractiveness affected the value of the brand asset: Japanese Social Research, "The Effect of Brand Personality and Brand Identification on Brand Loyalty: Applying the Theory of Social Identification," Wiley Online Library, December 19, 2002, http://onlinelibrary.wiley.com/doi/10.1111/1468-5884.00177/full.

CHAPTER 7

195 "To be a true Harley...it has to be cool": Dexter Ford, "Future Shock: Whispering Harleys," *New York Times*, June 19, 2014, http://www.nytimes.com/2014/06/22/automobiles/auto reviews/future-shock-whispering-harleys.html.

206 Legendary head coach Joe Paterno led the Penn State Nittany Lions from 1966 to 2011: "Penn State Child Sex Abuse Scandal," Wikipedia, https://en.wikipedia.org/wiki/Penn _State_child_sex_abuse_scandal.

207 the survey research firm Wilson Perkins Allen Opinion conducted a poll of over 1,000 adults: Wilson Perkins Allen Opinion, "Exclusive Polling Results," Framing of Joe Paterno, http://framingpaterno.com/exclusive-polling-results.

207 "Truth is stranger than fiction, but it is because Fiction is obliged to stick to possibilities; Truth isn't": Mark Twain, *Following the Equator: A Journey Around the World* (American Publishing Company, 1897).

217 I'd like you to watch a video on YouTube: Daniel Simons, "Selective Attention Test," YouTube, March 10, 2010, https://www.youtube.com/watch?v=vJG698U2Mvo.

217 Joachim de Posada, author of *Don't Eat the Marshmallow—Yet!*: Joachim de Posada and Ellen Singer, *Don't Eat the Marshmallow—Yet! The Secret to Sweet Success in Work and Life* (New York: Berkley Books, 2005)

CHAPTER 8

227   "three largest forces on the planet—globalization, Moore's law and Mother Nature": Thomas L. Friedman, "The Age of Protest," *New York Times*, January 13, 2016, http://www.nytimes.com/2016/01/13/opinion/the-age-of-protest.html.

227   "The economy has been changing in profound ways": "President Obama's Final State of the Union Address," NPR, January 12, 2016, http://www.npr.org/2016/01/12/462831088/president-obama-state-of-the-union-transcript.

235   "Leave it alone! It's great, and right on target!": "Commonly Asked Questions (and Answers)," Marshall McLuhan, http://www.marshallmcluhan.com/common-questions.

CHAPTER 9

250   In his book *Outliers*, Malcolm Gladwell suggests that it requires roughly 10,000 hours of practice to achieve mastery: Malcolm Gladwell, *Outliers* (Boston: Little, Brown and Company, 2008).

260   After all, we needed to sell Miami when *Time* magazine's cover story called our community "Paradise Lost": "Paradise Lost," *Time*, November 23, 1981, http://content.time.com/time/covers/0,16641,19811123,00.html.

265   "Life is an endless unfolding": John W. Gardner, "Personal Renewal, Delivered to McKinsey & Company, Phoenix, AZ, November 10, 1990," PBS, http://www.pbs.org/johngardner/sections/writings_speech_1.html.

265   "The only stability possible is stability in motion": John W. Gardner, *Self-Renewal, the Individual, and the Innovative Society* (New York: W. W. Norton & Company, 1964).

INDEX